Solidarity and Public Goods

In the wake of health and economic crises across the world, solidarity is emerging as both a moral imperative and urgent social goal. This book approaches solidarity as a political good, both a framework of power structures and grounds for moral motivation. The distinct approaches to public goods and social value demonstrate how social connectedness is intricately tied to the distribution of public goods, and the moral commitments that grow out of them.

The essays in this book explore different features of the political, moral and civic approaches to solidarity. They offer moral justification for solidarity, grounded in the intrinsic value of social connectedness and epistemic deference; propose structural accounts of solidarity as action against racial oppression, or as an effective non-moral framework; propose to redefine property relations, so as to capture and redistribute property's social value, and envision public goods as both an instrument of civic relations and as a condition to well-rounded, meaningful human lives. By providing a series of thought-provoking debates about social obligations and justice, the book re-establishes solidarity and public goods as an urgent and timely topic.

The chapters in this book were originally published as a special issue of the journal *Critical Review of International Social and Political Philosophy*.

Avigail Ferdman is Environmental Policy Fellow at the Israel National Economic Council where she works on climate change policy. She focuses on the philosophical and social conditions for meaningful human lives. Her work on human well-being, disruptive technologies, public goods and active mobility has been published in philosophy and planning journals.

Margaret Kohn is Professor of Political Theory at the University of Toronto, Canada. Her primary research interests are the history of political thought, critical theory, social justice and urbanism. She is the author of *The Death and Life of the Urban Commonwealth; Radical Space: Building the House of the People* and *Brave New Neighborhoods: The Privatization of Public Space*.

Solidarity and Public Goods

Edited by
Avigail Ferdman and Margaret Kohn

LONDON AND NEW YORK

First published 2021
by Routledge
2 Park Square, Milton Park, Abingdon, Oxon, OX14 4RN

and by Routledge
52 Vanderbilt Avenue, New York, NY 10017

Routledge is an imprint of the Taylor & Francis Group, an informa business

© 2021 Taylor & Francis
Chapter 7 © 2017 Rutger Claassen. Originally published as Open Access.

With the exception of Chapter 7, no part of this book may be reprinted or reproduced or utilised in any form or by any electronic, mechanical, or other means, now known or hereafter invented, including photocopying and recording, or in any information storage or retrieval system, without permission in writing from the publishers. For details on the rights for Chapter 7, please see the chapter's Open Access footnote.

Trademark notice: Product or corporate names may be trademarks or registered trademarks, and are used only for identification and explanation without intent to infringe.

British Library Cataloguing in Publication Data
A catalogue record for this book is available from the British Library

ISBN 13: 978-0-367-55180-3

Typeset in Myriad Pro
by Newgen Publishing UK

Publisher's Note
The publisher accepts responsibility for any inconsistencies that may have arisen during the conversion of this book from journal articles to book chapters, namely the inclusion of journal terminology.

Disclaimer
Every effort has been made to contact copyright holders for their permission to reprint material in this book. The publishers would be grateful to hear from any copyright holder who is not here acknowledged and will undertake to rectify any errors or omissions in future editions of this book.

Contents

	Citation Information	vi
	Notes on Contributors	viii
1	The theory and politics of solidarity and public goods *Avigail Ferdman and Margaret Kohn*	1
2	Solidarity as environmental justice in brownfields remediation *Avery Kolers*	10
3	Why should we care about competition? *Waheed Hussain*	26
4	Racial structural solidarity *Mara Marin*	42
5	What undermines solidarity? Four approaches and their implications for contemporary political theory *Charles H. T. Lesch*	57
6	Solidarity and social rights *Margaret Kohn*	72
7	Justice as a claim to (social) property *Rutger Claassen*	87
8	Engaging the reluctant taxpayer *Michael Joel Kessler*	102
9	Why the intrinsic value of public goods matters *Avigail Ferdman*	117
	Index	133

Citation Information

The chapters in this book were originally published in the *Critical Review of International Social and Political Philosophy*, volume 21, issue 5 (2018). When citing this material, please use the original page numbering for each article, as follows:

Chapter 1
The theory and politics of solidarity and public goods
Avigail Ferdman and Margaret (Peggy) Kohn
Critical Review of International Social and Political Philosophy, volume 21, issue 5 (2018), pp. 545–553

Chapter 2
Solidarity as environmental justice in brownfields remediation
Avery Kolers
Critical Review of International Social and Political Philosophy, volume 21, issue 5 (2018), pp. 554–569

Chapter 3
Why should we care about competition?
Waheed Hussain
Critical Review of International Social and Political Philosophy, volume 21, issue 5 (2018), pp. 570–585

Chapter 4
Racial structural solidarity
Mara Marin
Critical Review of International Social and Political Philosophy, volume 21, issue 5 (2018), pp. 586–600

Chapter 5

What undermines solidarity? Four approaches and their implications for contemporary political theory
Charles H. T. Lesch
Critical Review of International Social and Political Philosophy, volume 21, issue 5 (2018), pp. 601–615

Chapter 6

Solidarity and social rights
Margaret Kohn
Critical Review of International Social and Political Philosophy, volume 21, issue 5 (2018), pp. 616–630

Chapter 7

Justice as a claim to (social) property
Rutger Claassen
Critical Review of International Social and Political Philosophy, volume 21, issue 5 (2018), pp. 631–645

Chapter 8

Engaging the reluctant taxpayer
Michael Joel Kessler
Critical Review of International Social and Political Philosophy, volume 21, issue 5 (2018), pp. 646–660

Chapter 9

Why the intrinsic value of public goods matters
Avigail Ferdman
Critical Review of International Social and Political Philosophy, volume 21, issue 5 (2018), pp. 661–676

For any permission-related enquiries please visit:
www.tandfonline.com/page/help/permissions

Notes on Contributors

Rutger Claassen, Department of Philosophy and Religious Studies, Utrecht University, the Netherlands.

Avigail Ferdman, National Economic Council, Jerusalem, Israel.

Waheed Hussain, Department of Philosophy, University of Toronto, Canada.

Michael Joel Kessler, Trinity College, University of Toronto, Canada.

Margaret Kohn, Department of Political Science, University of Toronto, Canada.

Avery Kolers, Department of Philosophy, University of Louisville, KY, USA.

Charles H. T. Lesch, Department of Political Science, Hebrew University of Jerusalem, Israel.

Mara Marin, Department of Political Science, University of Victoria, Canada.

The theory and politics of solidarity and public goods

Avigail Ferdman ⓘD and Margaret (Peggy) Kohn

ABSTRACT
For over forty years, economic inequality and distributive justice have been two of the primary concerns of political philosophers. This volume addresses these issues in a novel way, by focusing on the concepts of solidarity and public goods as both descriptive and normative frameworks. Solidarity links the social, political and moral together, in a distinctively political approach that recognizes the social sources of power on the one hand and sources of moral motivation on the other. Public goods such as education, healthcare, and transport systems are indispensable to the forging of solidarity, but at the same time they may become sources of oppression or injustice, when they fail to respect individual autonomy or when they calcify majoritarian preferences. The essays in this volume explore different features of the political, moral and civic approaches to solidarity. The moral theory of solidarity is advanced in one case as an intrinsically valuable concept of social connectedness and in another as an approach of epistemic deference; a structural account of solidarity theorizes about action against racial oppression, and a power-relations account points at the urgency of the affective, non-rational dimensions of solidarity. The social value of property and its moral implications are articulated through the lens of French 19th Century 'Solidarism' and as a complementary theory to left-libertarianism. Public goods are defended as instrumental to solidarity, in one case within a liberal framework and in another within a human-perfectionism framework. By providing a series of thought-provoking debates about social obligations and justice, the volume re-establishes solidarity and public goods as pertinent concepts for theorizing about social justice and inequality.

The publication of Thomas Piketty's best-selling book *Capital in the twenty-first Century* sparked a global discussion about rising economic inequality. The growing concentration of wealth and income was already well known, but Piketty provided strong evidence to support several additional claims. First, he showed that inequality had reached levels similar to the era of the robber barons or what the French called the *Belle Époque*. Second, he argued that the equalization achieved in the first half of the twentieth century was anomalous and unlikely to recur without a politics of redistribution. Finally, he demonstrated that public wealth had been decimated and replaced by private wealth.

This volume addresses these issues, but it does so in a novel way, by focusing on the concepts of solidarity and public goods. For over forty years, economic inequality and distributive justice have been two of the primary concerns of political philosophers. While it would be unfair to fault political theory for the failures of political practice, it is worth asking why egalitarian political philosophy has not resonated in public discourse. In the *Belle Époque,* a largely forgotten group of French intellectuals asked a similar question. The philosopher Alfred Fouilleé worried that the abstract universalism of Kantian philosophy had failed to clarify the relationship between formal and substantive equality and had proved unable to motivate citizens to respond to urgent social problems. In order to address these concerns, the Radical Republicans, led by Léon Bourgeois, introduced the concept of solidarity. Solidarity was intended as a reinterpretation of the third principle of the famous slogan of the French revolution: liberty, equality, and fraternity. For the Radical Republicans, solidarity provided a way to justify the provision of public goods and to overcome the tension between liberty and equality.

Today, the concept of solidarity is not widely used by political theorists, and, at least in North America, it plays only a marginal role in public life. One challenge is that the term solidarity can be used in very different ways. The term is French in origin. According to the 1765 *Encyclopédie Commercial,* the term solidarity had a distinctive legal meaning. *Solidarité* referred to the obligation of a group of borrowers to discharge the debt of others (Brunkhorst, 2005). It was taken up by Auguste Comte and other sociologists who used it to describe the cohesiveness of a group (Metz, 1999). Solidarity has also played an important role in Catholic theology. Since the mid-twentieth century, it has been one of the primary principles of Catholic Social Teaching, where it describes the individual and collective obligation to help those in need (Scholz, 2008).

In her book *Political Solidarity*, Sally Scholz distinguishes between political, social, and civic solidarity. Social solidarity is the bond between members of a community united by shared characteristics. Civic solidarity implies reciprocal obligations among members of a political community to protect the vulnerable. Political solidarity is the term that she uses to describe the relations between members of a social movement or activist group, but it involves something more than just mutuality and cooperation among members of the group. It also entails a moral relationship to the cause itself and a set of obligations to the larger society (2008, p. 13). The primary duty is activism aimed at transforming the structural relations that produce injustice. While these three forms of solidarity differ, they also share some important features. All forms of solidarity are ways to mediate between the individual and the group. Solidarity binds people together, but it does so without giving absolute priority to the individual or the group. Most significantly, solidarity is a moral relationship that involves positive obligations (2008, p. 19).

This preliminary analysis helps us identify some of the promising and perhaps also problematic features of solidarity. Solidarity links the social, political, and moral together. It also provides an alternative framework that addresses some of the critiques of ideal theory. It is a distinctively political approach that recognizes the social sources of power and therefore provides a more adequate account of political action. The social ties among groups of activists or citizens can help solve the problem of moral motivation and explain why it is necessary to place the needs of others ahead of one's own interests. When members of a group have high levels of interdependence, they are more willing to prioritize the needs of others or to see interests as collective. This provides a way for the powerless to partially overcome asymmetries of power, but social solidarity can also be a source of injustice. The solidarity among members of political groups such as the Klu Klux Klan can serve unjust ends and mutual aid, and cooperation among privileged actors can exacerbate rather than mitigate inequality. As several contributors to this volume insist, solidarity must draw on and not replace normative theory.

This volume also contributes to the emerging literature on solidarity by exploring the relationship between solidarity and public goods. One of the most pressing, yet unacknowledged, problems in distributive justice is the need to account for the distribution of public goods. Standard approaches (Dworkin, 2000; Rawls, 1999) either neglect public goods or treat them as private goods (Vallentyne, Steiner, & Otsuka, 2005). Rousseau argued that public goods like festivals and civic spaces play a crucial role in fostering the solidarity among citizens that it makes it possible to reconcile equality and freedom. For liberal theorists, on the other hand, the provision of public goods poses a distinctive challenge. Why should the state force everyone to pay for goods that are preferred by some but not all citizens? Barring a few extreme cases (like national security), the decision whether to supply these goods as *public* goods – free of charge and non-exclusionary – is a political decision, which requires explicit moral justification (Miller and Taylor in press). This is especially important in the case of *non-universal* public goods – goods that are not in everyone's basic interest.

The contributions to this volume explore different features of the political, moral, and civic approaches to solidarity. The papers advance, and in some cases transform, the dominant way of interpreting these concepts. The first two papers defend two different moral theories of solidarity: a theory of epistemic deference (Kolers) and an account of the noninstrumental value of social connectedness (Hussein). In his article, Waheed Hussein asks, 'Why Should We Care about Competition?' He argues that liberal democracies should place limits on the allocation of goods through competitive institutions. These limits are justified because of the threat that competitive institutions pose to the value of human sociability and in particular from the noninstrumental value of a form of social connectedness that he calls 'mutual affirmation.' This approach improves on the instrumental argument, which holds that excessively competitive institutions are morally defective because they impede the formation of a rich network of social attachments, which is necessary for maintaining just arrangements over time. Hussein also shows that these ideas provide the basis for a powerful argument in favor of social provisions for public goods – e.g. a strong public healthcare system moderates the stakes in labor market competition, preventing the competition from descending into a life or death struggle.

In 'Solidarity as Environmental Justice in Brownfields Remediation,' Avery Kolers focuses on the maldistribution of public bads, specifically the environmental degradation that blights and contaminates poor and minority communities. His paper poses a challenging question for the political theory of solidarity. According to Scholz, membership in a political group like the environmental justice movement requires both a moral commitment to the cause and a responsibility to cooperate to discharge collective responsibilities (2008, p. 85). What happens when these two obligations seem to conflict? In Louisville, the residents of the poor neighborhoods that were most directly affected by contamination opposed a remediation plan that was endorsed by experts and allied environmental justice activists. Kolers argues that a moral theory of solidarity requires 'action on another's terms' even if this means deference to judgements that one disagrees with.

Mara Marin's article also examines the politics of social movements against injustice. She theorizes solidarity in the context of racial oppression and offers a structural account of solidarity. The paper develops such a notion of solidarity in conversation with the views proposed by Tommie Shelby (2002, 2005) and Robert Gooding-Williams (2009). Against the idea that such solidarity requires a shared ethno-cultural identity, Tommie Shelby defends the 'common oppression view' of solidarity, based solely on the victims' shared condition of oppression. According to Shelby, all victims of racial oppression can be reasonably expected to endorse a set of principles that will move them to common action. By pointing to the highly controversial nature of claims made in politics, Robert Gooding-Williams sheds doubts on the idea that such principles exist. Defending a view of politics as action-in-concert, marked by reasonable disagreement, Gooding-Williams advances a non-foundational view of solidarity constituted through the controversy of politics rather than derived from pre-political commitments or interests. The problem with such a notion, however, is that it is unable to link the unjust structures to the political action, and thus, it is unable to effectively transform social reality. Drawing on Iris Young's notion of 'gender as seriality' (Young, 1997), Marin defends a notion of 'structural solidarity,' distinguished by its ability to direct action along material patterns of inequality and disadvantage, as a better notion of solidarity under structural and intersecting conditions of oppression.

In his article, Charles Lesch explores solidarity from a different perspective. Lesch asks 'What Undermines Solidarity?' and turns to the work of Rousseau, Kant, Durkheim, and Levinas to answer this question. He examines Rousseau and Kant's sophisticated accounts of social pathology and argues that both provide grounds for doubting the assumption that solidarity will emerge organically out of liberal–democratic political systems, as long as they are rational or deliberative. Rousseau and Kant show that every society has informal power relations in which some are dominant and others quiescent and, if left unchecked, these forms of dependence will create a dynamic that is ripe for exploitation, abuse, and domination. They will lead not only to macro-scale social instabilities, but also micro-scale cruelties. Lesch argues that these everyday forms of dependence are inimical to the social trust and respect that are needed for solidarity. They are not eliminable by shared political principles or deliberative practices alone. He concludes that research should pay more attention to the affective, non-rational, and esthetic dimensions of solidarity.

The next two papers address the social value of property and its moral implications. Margaret Kohn, in 'Solidarity and Social Rights,' provides a distinctive theoretical foundation for social rights grounded in French nineteenth-century 'Solidarism.' Social rights to land, housing, food/water, and development, despite gaining formal recognition in some countries, are yet to be fully constitutionalized and universally guaranteed. Kohn argues that this is no coincidence: it is a consequence of an inherent ambivalence within liberal theory toward the tension between social structure and individual right. The liberal approach lacks a convincing account of how social circumstances affect individual autonomy and therefore cannot provide a satisfying account of social rights. It ends up – counterintuitively – endorsing illegitimately intrusive mechanisms for distinguishing the unlucky from the lazy. Kohn shows that solidarism, which explicitly accounts for the creation of social value in property, possesses the theoretical resources to include both social structure and individual right. The important difference between solidarism and liberalism, with respect to rights, is ontological: according to the liberal approach, a person is an autonomous individual who reflects about the principles that would secure their autonomy given that they share the world with others. On the solidarist account, persons are born vulnerable and dependent. Social ties sustain us, and therefore, we should repair and strengthen them. This moral obligation stems more from the human condition of precarity and vulnerability than from individual autonomy. The normative implication is that we must use social wealth to promote the flourishing of all members of society. In solidarism, therefore, individual flourishing and social circumstances are complementary, thereby providing a coherent account of social rights.

In 'Justice as a Claim to (Social) Property,' Rutger Claassen is more skeptical as to the analytic distinction between solidarism and autonomy. Claassen is interested in the distinction between right-libertarianism, in which individual property claims are central to justice, left-libertarianism, and egalitarianism, in which property claims are derivative. Does solidarism exist outside of this analytic framework, as a distinct theory of property relations and justice? Claassen argues that solidarism in fact exists within this framework and as a close cousin of left-libertarianism. The motivation driving this analytic examination is an attempt to unpack the political allure of right-libertarianism, which has proved immensely successful in grounding the morality of capitalism. To the extent that egalitarian theories aim to promote social justice by demonstrating that they are morally superior to right-libertarianism, they have to provide a convincing account of property, personhood, and political community. Claassen argues that despite solidarism's aim to identify property claims as social claims and provide an alternative account to right-libertarianism, the underlying moral obligation in solidarism is nevertheless a non-property-based fundamental principle. This makes solidarism closer to left-libertarianism and egalitarianism, in which property claims are not fundamental. Ultimately, Claassen argues, the value of the wealth we hold is socially determined, but the conditions for becoming autonomous are also much more socially determined than we normally realize. In order to offer a robust alternative to right-libertarianism, both political rhetoric and the theorizing of social justice stand to gain from conceptualizing autonomy and social circumstances simultaneously.

The final two articles return to the issue of public goods, and this was raised by Hussein in the first contribution to the volume. Hussein argued that public provision of goods like health care decreases the stakes of competition for employment, which enables people to enjoy the noninstrumental good of mutual affirmation. Public goods are indeed indispensable, yet the range of these goods is potentially vast; they range from religious amenities, through cultural preservation, transportation systems, conservation areas, to support for the arts. Citizens are often required, coercively, to collectively subsidize these goods even though they may not have any use for them. However, precisely because they do not accord with everyone's preferences and are not in everyone's direct self-interest, distributive equality in non-universal public goods may actually promote *in*justice. Justifying this sort of state coercion is even more urgent in multicultural and fragmented societies, where citizens will not be willing to cross-subsidize each other. In his paper, 'Engaging the Reluctant Taxpayer,' Michael Kessler notes that it is a central tenet of liberalism that citizens have a legitimate complaint when the coercive power of the state is used to promote a specific conception of the good. He examines this argument by focusing on the case of public funding for the arts. He develops an account that affirms the distinct value of the arts yet is still consistent with the liberal commitment to neutrality. He does this by showing how the arts can support just relations between citizens.

In the final paper, Avigail Ferdman challenges the 'liberal neutrality' framework that Kessler adopts. She argues that in order to achieve a comprehensive account of the distribution of public goods, we need to replace state-neutrality toward conceptions of the good life with an approach that explicitly accounts for intrinsic value. According to Ferdman, state-neutrality is conceptually inappropriate as a way to approach the question of public goods. Neutrality is a duty of the state in relation to private ends (Nagel, 1987), but the state cannot be neutral about its own ends. How then do we ensure that the provision of public goods does not further disadvantaged minorities? Some scholars suggest that the values of fairness and even-handed treatment can help, but Ferdman argues that an answer emerges if we reject the preference-based approach in favor of an account that recognizes intrinsic value. The criterion for judging when a thing has intrinsic value is derived from human flourishing theories (Hurka, 1993; Sher, 1997). According to Ferdman, non-universal public goods do more than merely allocate financial resources. They shape citizens, foster affective ties, and build solidarity. They perform an important role in creating and upholding the institutions through which we come to shape, revise, and change our conceptions of the good life and our conceptions of human flourishing.

Taken together, the contributions to the volume take up the unfinished project started by the solidarists almost one hundred and fifty years ago. This does not mean that the contributors all agree about the meaning of solidarity and the justification of public goods. What we see in this volume is a series of thought-provoking debates about the things that enable us to act together on behalf of ideals and the factors that prevent us from doing so. A careful analysis also reveals the Janus faces of some seemingly benign ideals. Solidarity can motivate people to help one another and to act collectively to combat structural injustice, but it also raises questions about power relations within groups and moral concerns about obligations to outsiders. The collective enjoyment of public goods may foster solidarity, but it can also lead to a systematic bias against minorities, inadequate provision of public goods, or illegitimate state coercion in the form of unjustified use of tax payers' money. The contributors engage in rigorous normative analysis, but they also take seriously the politics of equality. If Piketty is right, and the overwhelming destructiveness of the two world wars was the leading factor in dismantling the concentration of wealth in the *Belle Époque*, then we need creative theorizing and a public language that supports a transformative political project. The public good and solidarity are concepts that have been discredited by neoliberalism and overlooked by political philosophy. We hope this volume may foster an on-going conversation about their significance.

Acknowledgments

These papers were originally presented at a workshop on 'Public Goods and Solidarity' at the Centre for Ethics at the University of Toronto. The Editors would like to thank the Social Sciences and Humanities Research Council of Canada for its generous financial support.

Disclosure statement

No potential conflict of interest was reported by the authors.

Funding

This work was supported by Social Sciences and Humanities Research Council of Canada.

ORCID

Avigail Ferdman http://orcid.org/0000-0002-0950-8762

References

Brunkhorst, H. (2005). *Solidarity: From civic friendship to a global legal community*. Cambridge: MIT Press.

Dworkin, R. (2000). *Sovereign virtue*. Cambridge, MA: Harvard University Press.

Gooding-Williams, R. (2009). *In the shadow of Du Bois: Afro-modern political thought in America*. Cambridge, MA: Harvard University Press.

Hurka, T. (1993). *Perfectionism*. New York, NY: Oxford University Press.

Metz, K. H. (1999). Solidarity and history. Institutions and social concepts of solidarity in 19th century Western Europe. In K. Bayertz (Ed.), *Solidarity* (pp. 191–207). Dordrecht: Springer.

Miller, D., & Taylor, I. (in press). Distributive justice and public goods. In S. Olsaretti (Ed.), *The Oxford handbook of distributive justice*. Oxford: Oxford University Press.

Nagel, T. (1987). Moral conflict and political legitimacy. *Philosophy & Public Affairs, 16*(3), 215–240.

Piketty, T. (2014). *Capital in the twenty-first century*. Cambridge, MA: Belknap Press.

Rawls, J. (1999). *A theory of justice* (Revised Ed.). Cambridge, MA: Harvard University Press.

Scholz, S. J. (2008). *Political solidarity*. University Park: Penn State University Press.

Shelby, T. (2002). Foundations of black solidarity: Collective identity or common oppression? *Ethics, 112*(2), 231–266.

Shelby, T. (2005). *We who are dark: The philosophical foundations of black solidarity.* Cambridge, MA: Harvard University Press.

Sher, G. (1997). *Beyond neutrality: Perfectionism and politics.* Cambridge: Cambridge University Press.

Vallentyne, P., Steiner, H., & Otsuka, M. (2005). Why left-libertarianism is not incoherent, indeterminate, or irrelevant: A reply to Fried. *Philosophy & Public Affairs, 33*(2), 201–215.

Young, I. M. (1997). *Intersecting voices: Dilemmas of gender, political philosophy, and policy.* Princeton, NJ: Princeton University Press.

Solidarity as environmental justice in brownfields remediation

Avery Kolers

ABSTRACT

What do individuals owe to affected communities in the name of environmental justice? Principal accounts of environmental justice have made inroads in developing a pluralistic and activist-led approach. Yet precisely because of their strengths, such accounts face three problems – *indeterminacy*, *epistemology*, and *structure/agency* – that hinder activism and widespread engagement and threaten to leave 'every neighborhood for itself.' The current article examines an effort at brownfields remediation in Louisville, Kentucky, asking where environmental justice lies and how individuals ought to be engaged. Activist-led environmental justice cannot guide action, so the article defends a principle of solidarity as equity. Such solidarity requires individual engagement and, in the Louisville case, opposition to the proposed brownfields remediation plan.

Introduction

If states and social structures should receive credit for producing and distributing public goods, they must also be accountable for producing or maldistributing public *bads*. Among the latter are so-called brownfields – specific sites of environmental degradation that blight and contaminate their surrounding neighborhoods and burden the residents – and my concern here is principally with city-level efforts to rectify these harms.

It is by now widely agreed that cities and other public entities ought to restore brownfields, and that their efforts to do so must be undertaken in a context of thoroughgoing engagement with affected communities (Davies, 1999). Such inclusion is a hallmark of 'the quest for environmental justice' (Bullard, 2005). Yet implementing community inclusion itself raises problems of justice. First, community boundaries may be unclear – particularly if some residents have moved away to escape the environmental harms in question – and the members of communities may be divided among themselves. Cities have considerable power to elevate compliant voices and marginalize dissident ones. Second, the demand that state agencies and public entities practice inclusion, though correct so far as it goes, lets private individuals, particularly those in wealthier neighborhoods, off the hook. Environmental justice requires *activism*, and private individuals may be called upon to participate as activists. In the current paper, I shall argue that a principle for activism – solidarity with those who suffer inequity – plays an essential role in the quest for environmental justice in brownfields remediation. Specifically, such solidarity makes a demand upon private individuals even when they are completely innocent regarding the environmental burden in question. And it demands that private individuals leave aside questions of the content of environmental justice and take sides on the basis of structural position within a dispute. We must side with the victims of inequity.

Environmental justice (EJ) theory has its origins in academics' efforts to understand and support environmental justice activism. A distinctive and increasingly central aspect of this literature is the methodological commitment that theories of justice are responsible to activists on the ground who are doing the work of justice and anti-racism. By 'responsible' I mean not merely that theorists are trying to develop an account of justice for activists to use, but that EJ theories also seek to be *of* and *by* activists themselves. Theorists are in many cases also participants (Bullard, 2005; Schlosberg, 2007, 2013; Shrader-Frechette, 2002). EJ theorists are 'movement intellectuals' in a way that philosophers and social scientists more often refuse to be.

The activist-led character of EJ theory has yielded important insight, much of which has implications for theories of justice more broadly. But its most compelling features also generate three problems that I shall suggest can be resolved by adding an explicit principle of solidarity – in a sense I shall explain and defend – to accounts of environmental justice. I shall first lay out the key elements of activist-led environmental justice theory, drawing principally from the work of David Schlosberg. I shall then explain these three problems – plurality, epistemology, and institutional mediation – and illustrate them through a case study of a particular EJ struggle in Louisville, Kentucky. I will then argue that solidarity overcomes these problems.

The justice of environmental justice

Schlosberg (2007, 2013) has developed an approach to environmental justice that is explicitly activist-led and (consequently) pluralistic. He develops the theory by building inductively from EJ movements' words and deeds, as well as the work of engaged political theorists, and finally developing four irreducible principles of EJ. These four principles are *distribution, recognition, participation*, and *community capabilities*.

Philosophers have foregrounded distribution as the core, if not the entirety, of social justice. An appropriate distribution principle requires the absolute reduction of environmental burdens and the fair division of such burdens and benefits as are produced. But as Schlosberg (2007) – building on the work of Iris Marion Young, Nancy Fraser, and others – points out, maldistribution does not happen in a vacuum; still less does the redistribution that justice requires. Consequently, activists tend to downplay distribution per se as an EJ principle. Schlosberg's second and third principles, recognition and participation, speak to this dissonance by insisting that people be included and respected in decision-making processes, and not just at the moment of decision but all the way upstream at the stage of envisioning the values by which a society ought to be organized (Schlosberg, 2007; Shrader-Frechette, 2002). Recognition is both an individual psychological need for affirmation of oneself as worthy of respect and inclusion, and a structural demand that those who have been victimized be affirmed as having a valued place as equals in the larger society. A recognition principle thus addresses not merely the basic structure of society but its social mores and social group formation (Schlosberg). The fourth, community capabilities, principle expands upon Martha Nussbaum's (2006) list of basic human capabilities by explicating the capabilities of communities. Such capabilities include those of building and sustaining institutions and values, and bring into focus the environmental underpinnings of community flourishing – for instance, that the soil in which we grow our gardens is not contaminated, that our water isn't poisoning us, and so on (Schlosberg, 2007).

I think this activist-led orientation is broadly correct and adds important sophistication to the theory of justice. Its plural foundations reflect the real lived world of injustice and racism. Its emphasis on recognition and participation respects some of the most grinding features of environmental injustice and racism. And the appeal to community capabilities reflects the essentially structural character of much injustice, while also emphasizing that, often, things must get better all together if they are to get better at all. Nonetheless, precisely these strengths generate three fundamental problems for this activist-led approach:

> *Indeterminacy:* Although the plurality of the principles of justice is an important activist-led innovation, this very plurality makes it difficult to set a course of action when principles conflict. EJ might end up being either silent or self-contradictory.

> *Epistemology:* EJ activists typically face not just structural and physical but epistemological barriers to justice, and these barriers make it particularly difficult to recruit support from beyond the affected communities themselves. Social injustice and racism generate what Miranda Fricker (2007, pp. 17, 148) calls both *testimonial* and *hermeneutical* injustices. That is, because EJ activists emerge from marginalized communities, their factual claims tend to be dismissed more easily,

and they suffer a credibility deficit. They are often less able to marshal scientific resources to verify their claims or legal resources to make those claims actionable. Articulating their problems requires concepts or norms that are not broadly accepted in the larger society. All of these factors generate excess uncertainty about the existence and character of environmental injustices, as well as appropriate solutions. Even well-meaning observers might be inclined to step back from what they regard as factually dubious claims and wait until some established – usually white-led – organization, a university researcher, or the government weighs in.

Structure/agency: Third, because environmental injustices arise from massively distributed causal processes, (private) individuals rarely see themselves as implicated, nor could they plausibly be held culpable. It is therefore difficult to ground any stringent duties to contribute to EJ movements. Hence, EJ activism comes across as either *collective self-interest* (for the victims) or *morally optional* (for others).

These problems are mutually reinforcing. *Indeterminacy* can cause observers and even affected communities to disagree about whether justice lies in supporting or opposing some development; this feeds into the *Epistemology* problem, as internal disagreement and epistemic injustice push all parties to seek and rely upon the testimony of outside experts, rather than of activists on the ground; if each side coalesces around its own sympathetic experts, the competition between credentials and disciplines perversely further empowers outside experts relative to affected populations. And of course, uncertainty becomes a rationale for hanging back and not joining the struggle – especially when, due to the *structure/agency* problem, individuals feel no stringent duty to join up. All together, then, these problems exacerbate injustice and further marginalize the EJ activists whom the theory was supposed to be built to support.

Louisville's methane

It is tempting to imagine that these three mutually reinforcing, interlinked problems are merely theoretic; that in all real cases, the facts will be clear and the motivation to fight for justice will be abundant. Unfortunately, this is wishful thinking, as I will show by analyzing the case of two methane bio-digesters proposed for the west end of Louisville, Kentucky.[1]

In early 2015, a group of local investors, with high-level backing from Louisville's moderate Democratic mayor and liberal Democratic congressman, unveiled their plans to build a 'FoodPort' on a brownfield site in underdeveloped and predominantly African American west Louisville. The FoodPort was to be a spur to the local food economy, a place where local farmers, processors, chefs, and retailers could meet and overcome transaction costs and other competitive disadvantages against larger and typically out-of-state actors who extract profits but do not otherwise build the local economy.[2] Even better, it would contain a bio-digester that would capture methane from food waste and sell it to the electric utility for electricity generation. Landfills account for 20% of total US annual methane emissions – some 160 million metric tons of carbon dioxide equivalent per year (United States Environmental Protection Agency [USEPA], 2016). Methane, the second-most-prevalent greenhouse gas, constitutes about 10% of total emissions but is 25 times more potent than carbon dioxide. So the bio-digester promised to not only save landfill space but reduce greenhouse-gas emissions.[3] Finally, the FoodPort was to be located in a region that was not only desperate for investment and good jobs, but close to the heart of the local food desert.

In short, it should have been a huge win for the good guys. It was billed as a game-changer for west Louisville. It combined environmental aims with localism and, or so it seemed, environmental justice: It would remediate a brownfield in the west end and replace it with green businesses and green jobs available to the residents of the immediate area.

There was just one problem. The big day of the announcement seems to have been the first time many in the neighborhood had heard of it. The liberal establishment had air-dropped a rescue package on people who had not been consulted in advance about what they wanted, where, when, and how. Ownership of the site was not cooperative and not up for negotiation; shares were not offered to local residents. Nor did neighbors have a say in who the Food Port's tenants would be. Finally, residents who had suffered decades of chemical toxicity in their air and soil were outraged that a 'methane plant' was to be added to their community.

West Louisville is just downwind from two coal plants (one now converted to natural gas) along with their ash piles, and a web of chemical plants, called Rubbertown, dating to World War II. An old dump, unlined, poorly capped, and littered with toxic waste, abuts the Ohio River in west Louisville. For decades, an old pesticide plant leaked into people's yards, contaminating their soil and their homes. Over and above all these actual environmental blights are the environmental risks, and west Louisville bears more than its share of risk, too. Together, the maldistribution of burdens and risks has been deadly to fenceline communities while making it either impossible or immoral for homeowners to sell their homes, trapping them where they are. Not, of course, that they should have to leave, but for good reasons and bad, neither private nor government money has been available to clean up properly.

It was in the context of this long history of environmental injustice that the methane bio-digester proposal landed on west Louisville. Though its backers expected to be welcomed, many in the neighborhood understandably experienced it as an attack – all the more so when a local distillery proposed a second bio-digester in the area. Nonetheless, the FoodPort seemed to be win-win-win: good green jobs that could not go away; economic investment in a community that had suffered disinvestment; brownfields remediation; and reduction of carbon emissions. When the residents of west Louisville rose up to reject the methane plant, the plant's backers were just as surprised as the residents had been by the initial announcement. While the FoodPort entrepreneurs responded by at least temporarily shelving their bio-digester,[4] the distillery, with the help of the mayor, reached a Community Benefits Agreement (CBA) proposing to invest about $5 million in the neighborhood, principally benefiting two Historically Black educational institutions, Simmons College and Kentucky State University (Lopez, 2015). The CBA succeeded in winning over some critics, but the opponents charged them with having sold out. Protests did not stop, and when a city Zoning Board hearing refused to endorse the plan, the distillery eventually scrapped it with the intention of searching for another site.

The bio-digester case manifests the three problems laid out above. In a single-criterion theory of justice, it would be easy in principle to determine what policy *really* enhances justice by that theory's criterion. But Schlosberg's criteria generate indeterminacy by diverging on the question of which groups, institutions, or policies are most attractive. For instance, in west Louisville the bio-digester – particularly given the CBA – arguably would have reduced distributive injustice and enhanced some community capabilities, while failing on the recognition and participation criteria. So where does EJ lie? The obvious answer might seem to be, 'where the EJ activists are,' but we don't know which are the EJ activists unless we know what EJ is.

Second, the case generates several *epistemological* challenges. The two sides disagreed on whether the methane plant even counted as an environmental burden; its backers thought it was the opposite. A precautionary principle might prioritize the activists' concerns, but proponents were adamant that the associated risk was near zero; and anyway, many liberals object to precautionary principles on the grounds that they put a thumb on the cost/benefit scale (Broome, 2012).

Finally, normative and epistemic uncertainties give individuals a reason not to get involved – particularly when the injustices are not the fault of private individuals observing today. Even if they want to do their part for environmental justice, individuals can be expected to stick to what they know and to leave messy questions to others. In fact, not only is this course of reasoning to be *expected*, it seems from a liberal perspective to be *preferable*, since it hedges against the risk of harming people we do not know or understand (Broome, 2012, pp. 13–14Mill, 2002, p. 19). And yet this attitude generates an 'every neighborhood for itself' dynamic, which relatively disempowers those neighborhoods with the fewest resources and hence exacerbates environmental injustice.

Thus, if they are to help individuals overcome the indeterminacy, epistemology, and structure/agency problems, EJ theorists need a political theory of individual responsibility for environmental justice.

Individual responsibility for environmental justice

EJ theories have difficulty determining which side we should take in cases like the methane plant, where the core principles of environmental justice diverge. Yet even if the indeterminacy and epistemology problems were solved, EJ theorists would still face the challenge of grounding individual responsibilities to support EJ movements. Nor, unfortunately, is political philosophy an immediate source of solutions. Political philosophers tend to endorse an instrumental natural duty of justice on which everyone is required to uphold and support just institutions (Murphy, 2014; Rawls, 1999). Yet this instrumental duty is infamously underspecified in cases where claims of justice pull in competing directions. Worse, when there are multiple injustices – as there are in all nonideal contexts – then once again the epistemic uncertainty surrounding claims of environmental injustice will license liberals to focus on injustices that are more certain. The instrumental natural duty is therefore a nonstarter for resolving this question of individual responsibility.

Instead of the natural duty of justice, Kristen Shrader-Frechette (Shrader-Frechette, 2007, p.112) offers the following 'Responsibility Argument' for a duty of EJ activism:

(1) If some institutional order, like government, displays radical inequality in the degree to which citizens' human rights are fulfilled, this order is prima facie unjust (PFU), and consequently the burden of proof is on its defenders.

(2) If citizens (to varying degrees) regulate this PFU order, elect its leaders, and cooperate socio-economically in it, citizens are partly responsible for this prima facie injustice.

(3) If 1 and 2 are true, citizens must either defend this PFU order, withdraw from it, or compensate for the unfair benefits they gain from participation in it.

(4) If withdrawal from this unjust order is unrealistic, citizens must either defend it or compensate for their unfair benefits gained from it…

(5) If 3 and 4 are true, and [the only means to defend the PFU order all fail], the PFU order cannot be defended. To compensate for their benefits from it, citizens should work to stop injustice in this order.

Premise (1) is problematic because of its invocation of *radical inequality*. While it is clearly true that environmental injustices partly constitute larger global radical inequalities, it is less obvious that 'radical inequality' is applicable to environmental injustice per se, or still less, any particular environmental injustice. And, if an inequality is not *radical*, premise (1) does not say whether it is *prima facie* unjust.

Supposing we grant the existence of a prima facie injustice, however, premise (2) asserts what we might call 'citizenship responsibility' for this injustice

SOLIDARITY AND PUBLIC GOODS

(Pasternak, 2010). Shrader-Frechette intends this as a kind of backward-looking joint liability for the injustice; we have wronged others and are in their moral debt. The question is what that debt entails. Premise (3) presents three alternative courses of action – withdrawal, compensation, and defense. Premise (4) assumes that withdrawal is unrealistic and rules out defense,[5] leaving only compensation, as indicated in premise (5).

Unfortunately, Shrader-Frechette treats (5) as a conclusion requiring no further argument. But (5) adds something substantive to the argument, namely what we might call the *activism as compensation* thesis. Shrader-Frechette does not give any reason to think that activism can be explained or justified as compensation, and I believe that this way of thinking is fundamentally mistaken. Let us grant, for the sake of the argument, that citizen responsibility generates duties of compensation. It does not follow, however, that EJ activism is a means of compensating anyone. To the contrary, there are both normative and conceptual reasons to reject activism as compensation. The normative objection is that if compensation is owed, the victim should have a say in the form that it takes. Shrader-Frechette assumes that compensation should be given in the form of activism. Yet the victims might prefer that those who are liable just gave them cash equivalent to the excessive harms and risks they bear. Ironically, then, the compensation thesis commits the participatory injustice of failing to consult the victims about how they want to be compensated. This failing is evident in cases like the methane plant, where the bio-digester was *not implausibly* presented as a boon – as repairing underdevelopment and environmental injustice – but the neighbors were not consulted in a timely fashion about whether they wanted this putative benefit.

The conceptual problem with the activism as compensation thesis can be illustrated by imagining two agents, S and T, who contribute to two movements, M_1 and M_2, respectively. Suppose that the success of the respective movements would achieve 'full compensation,' and that M_1 fails, while M_2 succeeds. Hence, all and only the beneficiaries of M_2 are fully compensated; the intended beneficiaries of M_1 are not. Suppose S and T worked equally hard. It seems to follow that S's efforts are totally worthless, whereas T's completely discharge his obligations. S still owes just as much as she did before. That result seems unfair to S. Yet this may be too quick; for although M_2 was successful, T's individual contribution was likely superfluous, as is typical of individual contributions to successful social movements. Now, we might plausibly see T's contributions as also worthless, since bandwagon-jumpers cannot take credit for the direction or speed of the wagon. If superfluous contributions count, then the sum of all contributions is greater than the required compensation, and the beneficiaries of M_2 might now be thought to have received excess payback, and owe something back to T and his comrades. If contributions count based on causal impact, then neither S nor T has compensated anyone. If they count based on the effect of the movement, then all S's work is worthless. If they count based on the amount of work performed, then T's beneficiaries – and perhaps even S's – have been overcompensated. Each method of cashing out contributions seems unjust to someone, if not incoherent. These problems come from treating activism as compensation. Activism to fight injustice cannot be grounded in compensation of the victims of injustice.

This conclusion leaves a worrisome gap in EJ theory. Because of the indeterminacy, epistemology, and structure/agency problems, EJ theory cannot require any individual responsibility to contribute to EJ movements. Indeed, to the contrary, some important moral commitments, such as that one should not try to benefit people one doesn't understand or consult, seem to generate positive moral reasons *not* to contribute to EJ movements. But this result leaves us in a centripetal 'every-neighborhood-for-itself' dynamic, which merely exacerbates environmental injustice and racism. If environmental justice is to become a reality, we need to ground an individual responsibility to contribute to EJ movements even when those movements are in other people's backyards.

Solidarity

I believe that *solidarity*, and specifically, a conception of solidarity grounded in equity, can resolve these problems and ground this individual responsibility.

We need, first, a definition of solidarity. By 'solidarity' here I mean the solidarity that occurs when unions, social movements, and such join together to fight for political aims. A standard approach to such 'political solidarity' in the literature is to understand it *teleologically* as a joint action aimed toward a common goal (Sangiovanni, 2015; Shelby, 2005). Typically, and sometimes by definition, authors understand the goal to be *justice* or *alleviating oppression*. One ought to join in solidarity, then, if doing so is the most effective way to bring about justice; and if multiple paths toward justice exist, solidarity is morally optional. Teleological views thus treat solidarity, morally, as an extension of the instrumental natural duty of justice.

I have two principal relevant objections to teleological accounts: first, by presupposing that participants *antecedently* shared their goals – they come together to pursue these shared goals, rather than vice versa – teleological accounts prioritize individual conscience over group decision-making. Each agent's own judgment about who is on the side of the angels determines which side that agent should be on. But this is both unrealistic in social movements and unattractive in EJ cases characterized by indeterminacy and epistemic injustice. Second, teleological views are also silenced when the chances of success seem low, because then the project is unrealistic or irrational; recall that all of S's work, in the example above, was for naught. But nor is there much reason to contribute when the chances of success seem high, since after all T's contribution is superfluous. In either case – S works hard to achieve nothing; T works hard but makes no difference – the opportunity costs of participation are overwhelming, and hence, solidarity is unjustifiable. No movement can be built on this teleological foundation.

Departing from teleological accounts, *relational* approaches maintain the instrumental orientation but modulate it by situating solidarity within activist networks (Gould, 2014; Scholz, 2008). Each aspect – the orientation to justice and embeddedness in the relationship or network – is essential to solidarity. I worry, however, that the addition of networks sows only confusion. In the first instance, solidarity seems fundamentally to involve the unification of those who are not already joined together. Hence, whatever bounds the network has, solidarity must also include collaboration *beyond* those bounds. The relational approach cannot include this. At most, it might appeal to an independent reason to expand the bounds of the network. But if solidarity presupposes a network, then solidarity itself cannot ground any reason to expand the network or anyone's reason to join it.

Further, within any given network, the relational account risks circularity. For we must ask how the network is formed and how it settles on its views about where justice lies. If each member comes to the group already having an account of justice, and the network is composed of those who antecedently agree, then the relational approach collapses into the teleological approach: solidarity is when people who share a goal come together to pursue that goal. If, on the other hand, we imagine that an account of justice emerges from within the network, we must investigate the network's internal dynamics to determine how the convergence occurs. Given the internal disputes about where justice lies, it will be possible to appeal for solidarity *within* the network, as a reason for taking one view of justice as opposed to another. For instance, if, as occurred in west Louisville, a CBA selectively distributes benefits among community members, those who stand to benefit may disagree with others about whether to support the CBA. Then, members of the network might issue competing calls for solidarity *within* the network. If so, then the relational account is circular.

Against the teleological and relational approaches, I understand solidarity as *political action on others' terms*. The others may or may not be acting for justice; they may or may not be likely to succeed; the agent may or may not antecedently be in a relationship with them or agree with them. Unlike teleological and relational accounts, this 'deferential' approach implies that Nazis are just as capable of solidarity as anyone else; the question is not whether Nazis *can* be in solidarity, but whether they *ought* to be. And on pain of circularity, this latter question, the normative question, cannot be decided either by the agent's view about justice or their antecedent relationships. We do not, that is, find like-minded allies and work together for our antecedently shared vision of justice; contrariwise, we become of like mind, if we do, *because* we find one another and work together. The joining comes first.[6]

I should emphasize and clarify that this is a *conceptual* claim: solidarity is political action on others' terms. This conceptual claim has a methodological implication: solidarity cannot be justified by appeal to antecedent agreement (about, e.g. justice), because then the terms of our action would not be *others'* terms, but our own. And this methodological implication is normatively significant, because it rules out an otherwise plausible strategy for justifying solidarity. It follows that this deferential account must put all the justificatory weight onto the question of how we should pick sides in a political struggle: *to whom* we should defer.

While this normative question might be answered in a variety of ways, in my view the basic case for solidarity is grounded in *equity*. Equity is often associated with simple economic distribution. Indeed, this is how Schlosberg (2007) understands it in explicating his pluralistic approach to environmental justice, assuming that equity leaves out participation, recognition, and community capabilities. But equity is both more fundamental and more practical than economic justice alone. Equity is the core of justice – the recognition of each as an equal who is entitled to equal respect and basic fairness. May (2011) understands equity as encompassing the basic *Magna Carta* rights: *habeas corpus*, as well as the right to have one's charges read in public, to confront one's accuser, and not to be made an outlaw. Equity may similarly be understood as the 'natural' or 'pre-institutional' core of Kantian justice. Anna Stilz (2011) distinguishes between the natural right to equal authority and basic security of person, and all the other rights that we get in political society. Understood as the core of justice, what equity protects is each person's status as a full and equal member of a shared polity, or indeed, as David Wiggins (following Hume) suggests, of 'the party of humankind' (Wiggins, 2008, pp. 10–11).

Equity grounds solidarity in two respects. First, when someone calls for solidarity and we are forced to choose – either to cross the picket line or not; either to support the methane plant or not – we must take the side of those who are treated (most) inequitably within the scope of the relevant struggle. In taking their side, we countermand the inequity and thus treat them equitably. This is a constitutive relation, not a causal one. That is, solidarity might or might not *bring about* equitable treatment more broadly, for instance by winning the day for the victims and achieving equity. But even when the movement fails, solidarity *partly constitutes* equitable treatment. Equitable treatment is intrinsically valuable, and hence, solidarity with victims of inequity is intrinsically valuable when and because it constitutes equitable treatment of them. Here, we completely avoid the puzzle that undermined the compensation view; both S and T meet a duty of solidarity even though M_1 fails and T's contribution to M_2 is superfluous.

This first sense of equity as fundamental fairness is a property of social structures and entails that solidarity partly constitutes equitable treatment. This alone would make some action in solidarity intrinsically valuable because equity is intrinsically valuable and would make solidarity obligatory because treating people equitably is obligatory. Yet this first sense does not fully capture what is distinctive about solidarity as opposed to recognition or even a (noninstrumental) natural duty of justice. What is distinctive about solidarity is the way it commits the agent not only to justice as such but to particular others. It does so in two ways: First, by demanding political action not only for others' *benefit* but on their *terms*; hence, the agent in solidarity commits to defer to particular others' best judgment of what is to be done. Second, solidarity entails a commitment to *share their fate* in some normatively significant sense (Sangiovanni, 2015).

Being directly committed to others is a property of persons, rather than of social structures. A second sense of equity – Aristotle's notion of *being an equitable person* – captures this direct commitment. According to Aristotle, an equitable person is one 'who chooses and does [equitable] acts, and is no stickler for his rights in a bad sense but tends to take less than his share though he has the law on his side' (Aristotle, 2009, 1137b). Being an equitable person captures both aspects of the direct commitment that solidarity entails. Suppose that you and I are struggling together for our fair share of some public good. For some reason, I suddenly find myself in position to attain my own fair share of it – not by backstabbing or subterfuge, just by gaining access. Since this is my fair share, I have a right to get it; from the standpoint of justice, you have no legitimate criticism of my doing so. To the extent that I am an equitable person, however, I will not accept what is justly mine as long as such justice is denied to you. Rather, I will commit to share your fate, taking less than my share though I have justice on my side.

Now consider deference. Suppose I am in solidarity with you, and we disagree about where justice lies or what the best course of action is. I may be confident in my reasoning – that I have, as it were, 'the law on [my] side' – both the moral law and the laws of logic. Nonetheless, in solidarity with you I do not stand on my own but I 'choose and do equitable acts' by deferring to you, whose struggle it is. I need not defer at every moment; in strategy sessions, I will defend my views – but when action is required I will act as if with your hands and speak as if with your voice. Solidarity is acting as the other would if they could be in two places at once.

In both Kantian and Aristotelian senses, then, solidarity is equity.[7] Thus, in contrast to teleological solidarity, where we take our own view of justice as a goal and our own judgment about tactics as normative, in deontological solidarity, we take *the group's view* of justice *because they are victims of inequity*, and we commit to be equitable persons by sharing their fate. If the group is internally divided, we can apply this very same logic to choosing sides within the group. So unlike relational solidarity, solidarity-as-equity does not fall into circularity. Not only is this account not vitiated by the prospect of losing or by the lack of a prior relationship with those who struggle for justice, but it is most important precisely when they are losing and we aren't already connected.

The methane plant case gives us essentially two options. We can go with what is arguably the right answer from the standpoint of distributive justice and environmentalism, or we can go with what the least empowered people in the community say. We can follow an innovative development that seems to be win-win-win, or we can insist that that policy be shelved unless the people on the bottom have a decisive role in design and implementation. We can accept that the city and the developers have property rights in the brownfield that is to be redeveloped, or we can see that brownfield through the geographically and historically situated eyes of residents who have been dumped on for decades because they are largely poor and largely African American. Solidarity as equity endorses the latter side of each option.

I do not want to claim that Shrader-Frechette and Schlosberg *could not* reach similar results; to the contrary, I think these results are highly congenial to their activist-led EJ perspective. My claim is, rather, that solidarity as equity *entails* these results, whereas these other views fail to rule out the alternative. This is the case because the very pluralism of Schlosberg's theory opens the indeterminacy problem, whereas deontological solidarity closes it. Similarly, deference forestalls each agent's license to judge for himself whether the activists are right about what's best for them. And the intrinsic value of treating others equitably by being in solidarity with them grounds a duty to work alongside EJ movements that cannot be explained by appeal to compensation. Solidarity as equity is also broader than Shrader-Frechette's responsibility argument in that persons can suffer inequitable treatment even when they do not suffer from radical inequality, and because even noncitizens or those who are innocent of any injustice can have duties of solidarity.

The most challenging objection to solidarity as equity may be that deference is a dangerous and ultimately irrational externalization of each agent's own moral judgment, and if we practice deference, we may find ourselves committed to iniquitous actions that are made no more justifiable by the fact that they are carried out by victims of inequity. We risk helping the oppressed turn into oppressors.

I cannot here fully answer this charge, but I can emphasize that equity itself limits solidarity; one cannot act equitably *by* acting *in*equitably. As Wiggins (2008, p. 12) emphasizes, one function of solidarity – one sense in which it is fundamentally deontological – is precisely to forbid certain violations of others. Drawing on the work of Philippa Foot, Wiggins writes, 'a space surrounds another; and the preservation of that space forbids unprovoked injury, murder, plunder or pillage.' Solidarity treats equitably the victims of inequity, 'preserving that space' around them. It cannot on these grounds justify violating that space against others.

Conclusion

Schlosberg's activist-led EJ theory offers four irreducible principles of environmental justice: distribution, recognition, participation, and community

SOLIDARITY AND PUBLIC GOODS

capabilities. From the perspective of distribution and community capabilities, it seems that the loss of the methane bio-digesters in west Louisville may be a net negative. Unable to build on-site, the distillery will either have to give up on recycling organic waste or do so off-site, which would require trucking the waste from the distillery to the bio-digester. Pollution may consequently worsen. As for the FoodPort, the loss of the bio-digester in 2015 left it dependent on one particular tenant, and when that tenant pulled out in mid-2016, the FoodPort collapsed (Bailey & Bruggers, 2016). Although no replacement plan existed at the time, a new remediation plan has since been developed through a bottom-up process of proposals that came from the community itself" (City of Louisville 2017).

Opponents were successful in inserting the neighborhood's voice into a development process that often seems to see more back rooms than sunlight. They have called on the city to make available to the community the millions of dollars it found for the wealthy entrepreneurs behind the FoodPort. And they have insisted that west Louisville must not be treated as a dumping ground, where waste is processed for the rest of the city. City and state governments are developing regulations requiring that such plants remain a safe distance from residential property. These are victories for recognition and participation.

EJ theorists insist that distribution cannot be the sole principle of environmental justice, and the case of the methane bio-digesters bears this out. But plurality generates problems of indeterminacy, epistemology, and structure/agency that are not overcome by the emergence of an EJ movement or even by that movement's eventual success. Solidarity cuts through these challenges and calls upon us not to do what's right, but to support those who are treated inequitably. In doing so, we treat them equitably, irrespective of how things eventually turn out.

Notes

1. I am grateful to Lauren Heberle for helping with this case analysis.
2. For an overview, see McKenzie (2016).
3. Indeed, such bio-digesters are a significant part of the US strategy for meeting its Paris targets.
4. Downs (2015). The FoodPort idea was later scrapped altogether.
5. I leave aside the specifics of premise (4). I think that premise is problematic, but my argument here implies that the Responsibility Argument fails to require EJ activism even if we grant (4).
6. Solidarity as I understand it is a form of what Waheed Hussain (this volume) would call *affirmation*, but solidarity may be *unilateral* affirmation rather than *mutual* affirmation, and nor does it presuppose an antecedently shared common good. If *A* is in solidarity with *B*, then *A* unilaterally affirms *B*, and although *B* must somehow *accept* that affirmation (by, e.g. acknowledging *A*), *B* does not necessarily reciprocate it.

7. I have made this case at greater length in Kolers (2016), though the account here is more unified.

Acknowledgments

I am grateful to Lauren Heberle for reading and discussion of a prior draft and particularly for helping with the details of the case study, and to an anonymous referee for comments on a prior draft. I am also grateful to Peggy Kohn, Avigail Ferdman, and all the participants in the workshop on Public Goods, Solidarity, and Social Justice at the Centre for Ethics, University of Toronto, in May 2016.

Disclosure statement

No potential conflict of interest was reported by the author.

References

Aristotle. (2009). *Nicomachean ethics* (D. Ross, Trans.). In L. Brown (Ed.). New York, NY: Oxford University Press.

Bailey, P.M., & Bruggers, J. (2016, January 7). Methane plant plans for West Louisville killed. *Louisville Courier-Journal*. Retrieved from http://www.courier-journal.com/story/news/politics/metro-government/2016/01/07/fischer-pressed-drop-methane-plant-support/78403056/

Bailey, P. M., & Downs, J. (2016, August 18). Mayor: FoodPort 'too big' for some to grasp. *Louisville Courier-Journal*. Retrieved August 24, 2016, from http://www.courier-journal.com/story/news/local/2016/08/18/fischer-foodport-too-big-some-grasp/88923536/

Broome, J. (2012). *Climate matters*. New York, NY: Norton.

Bullard, R. D. (Ed.). (2005). *The quest for environmental justice*. San Francisco, CA: Sierra Club.

City of Louisville. 2017. "Mayor announces $30 million indoor track and field facility to be developed on Heritage West site." 19 September 2017. Retrieved 1 November 2017. https://louisvilleky.gov/news/mayor-announces-30-million-indoor-track-and-field-facility-be-developed-heritage-west-site

Davies, L. L. (1999). Working toward a Common Goal: Three case studies of Brownfields redevelopment in environmental justice communities. *Stanford Environmental Law Journal, 18*, 285–332.

Downs, J.. (2015, August 13). FoodPort drops idea for methane gas plant. *Louisville Courier-Journal*. Retrieved August 24, 2016, from http://www.courier-journal.com/story/news/local/centralwest/2015/08/13/west-louisville-foodport-plans-canceled/31620331/

Fricker, M. (2007). *Epistemic injustice*. New York, NY: Oxford University Press.

Gould, C. (2014). *Interactive democracy*. New York, NY: Cambridge University Press.

Hussain, W., this volume. Why should we care about competition?

Kolers, A. (2016). *A moral theory of solidarity*. New York, NY: Oxford University Press.

Lopez, A. (2015, November 5). West Louisville residents divided over $5 Million Biodigester deal. *WFPL News*. Retrieved August 12, 2016, from http://wfpl.org/west-louisville-residents-divided-over-5-million-biodigester-deal/

May, L. (2011). *Global justice and due process*. New York, NY: Cambridge University Press.

McKenzie, E. (2016). *Unholy cow: The complete history – so far – of plans to build a methane digester in west Louisville* [online]. Louisville, KY: Broken Sidewalk. Retrieved August 25, 2016, from http://brokensidewalk.com/2016/waste-to-energy-roundup/

Mill, J.S. (2002). *Utilitarianism*. In Sher, G. (Ed.). (2nd ed.). Indianapolis, IN: Hackett.

Murphy, L. (2014). *What makes law*. New York, NY: Cambridge University Press.

Nussbaum, M. C. (2006). *Frontiers of justice*. Cambridge, MA: Harvard University Press.

Pasternak, A. (2010). Sharing the costs of political injustices. *Politics, Philosophy, and Economics, 10*, 188–210.

Rawls, J. (1999). *A theory of justice* (revised ed.). Cambridge, MA: Harvard University Press.

Sangiovanni, A. (2015). Solidarity as joint action. *Journal of Applied Philosophy, 32*, 340–359.

Schlosberg, D. (2007). *Defining environmental justice*. New York, NY: Oxford University Press.

Schlosberg, D. (2013). Theorising environmental justice: The expanding sphere of a discourse. *Environmental Politics, 22*, 37–55.

Scholz, S. (2008). *Political solidarity*. University Park, PA: Penn State University Press.

Shelby, T. (2005). *We who are dark*. Cambridge, MA: Harvard University Press.

Shrader-Frechette, K. (2002). *Environmental justice*. New York, NY: Oxford University Press.

Shrader-Frechette, K. Human Rights and Duties to Alleviate Environmental Injustice: The Domestic Case . Journal of Human Rights. 2007; 6(1), 107–130.

Stilz, A. (2011). *Liberal loyalty*. Princeton, NJ: Princeton University Press.

United States Environmental Protection Agency. (2016). *US greenhouse gas inventory report: 1990–2014* (EPA-430-R-16-002) [online]. Washington, DC. Retrieved August 11, 2016, from https://www.epa.gov/sites/production/files/2016-04/documents/us-ghg-inventory-2016-main-text.pdf

Wiggins, D. (2008). Solidarity as the root of the ethical. *Lindley Lecture*. Lawrence, KS: University of Kansas.

Why should we care about competition?

Waheed Hussain

ABSTRACT
Most people believe that competitive institutions are morally acceptable, but that there are limits: a friendly competition is one thing; a life or death struggle is another. How should we think about the moral limits on competition? I argue that the limits stem from the value of human sociability, and in particular from the noninstrumental value of a form of social connectedness that I call 'mutual affirmation.' I contrast this idea with Rawls's account of social union and stability. Finally, I show how these ideas provide the basis for a powerful argument in favour of social provisions for public goods: for example, a strong public health care system moderates the stakes in labour market competition, preventing the competition from descending into a life or death struggle.

Many important social institutions tend to be competitive. Some examples include markets, democratic elections, adversarial systems of justice, and college admissions processes. A key feature of these institutions is that they 'pit people against each other': they put people in circumstances where the only way for one person to secure an important good is by formulating and successfully carrying out a plan that will effectively interfere with some other person's formulating and successfully carrying out a plan to secure an important good. For example, the typical mayoral election creates a situation in which for any one candidate to secure the office, she has to formulate and successfully carry out a plan that will effectively block all of the other candidates from securing the office.

Competitive institutions put people in situations where they must undermine one another as a necessary side effect of their pursuit of their own aspirations. There is something antisocial about these arrangements, and philosophical disagreements about the proper place of competitive institutions in a liberal democracy stem in part from different views about the nature and value of human sociability or social connectedness.

One view is broadly *instrumental*. It says that human beings form bonds of sympathy and attachment with one another, and that these bonds are important mainly because they help to ensure that people will treat one another as justice requires. The problem with competitive institutions, on this view, is that they impede the formation of social attachments and thereby undermine the motivational structures necessary for people to reliably treat one another in a just fashion.

The other view is broadly *noninstrumental*. It says that the members of a political community stand in a particular social relationship with one another. The political relationship, much like friendship or family relations, makes certain demands on how people should think and act (see Dworkin, 1986). Among these 'associative obligations' is a requirement that citizens should think and act in ways that constitute a kind of caring concern for one another. The political relationship requires a certain type of social connectedness among citizens and it prohibits excessively competitive institutions because these institutions are antithetical to the relevant form of connectedness.

In this paper, I want to develop the social democratic idea that competitive institutions are sometimes objectionable because they do not respect the noninstrumental value of social connectedness. My argument will focus on two questions: (1) how should we conceptualise the form of social connectedness that is distinctively important from the standpoint of political morality? and (2) how should we think about the value of social connectedness, so understood? The argument that I develop draws on the work of Ronald Dworkin (1986), Jean-Jacques Rousseau (1979, 1997a, 1997b) and Karl Marx (1964), and I will loosely contrast this argument with John Rawls's (1999) account of social union and his account of stability.

Let me note at the outset that my motivation for formulating the social democratic view is not to argue for some form of socialism. My goal is rather to contribute to a broader account of the proper place of competitive institutions in a liberal democracy. Most people agree that competitive institutions are acceptable up to a point. And most people agree that competition can go too far: a friendly competition is one thing; a life or death struggle is another. The noninstrumental value of social connectedness gives us a way of thinking about why liberal democracies may adopt competitive institutions, but why they must also moderate and contain the sphere of competition in social life. I will use the case of health insurance to illustrate the moral limits of competition.

Two conceptions of social connectedness

Let me distinguish first between two conceptions of social connectedness. The first conception is articulated in Rawls's idea of *social union*. In section 79 of *A Theory of Justice*, Rawls says that individuals achieve 'social union' when they are engaged in a certain kind of activity. Activities of this kind have two important features. First, there is a mutually recognised plan that defines various roles and assigns individuals to these roles. Second, each person does her part in the overall activity because the activity serves some objective that she values as a final end.

The example that Rawls uses to illustrate is an orchestra (Rawls, 1999, p. 459f4). In an orchestra, there is a mutually recognised musical score, which defines various roles for musicians, and an assignment of individuals to each role. Furthermore, each musician plays her part in the musical enterprise because the orchestral performance serves some objective that she values as a final end – for example, it realises her aspiration to make beautiful orchestral music.

What stands out about social union, from Rawls's point of view, is that in social union 'we cease to be mere social fragments' (1999, p. 464). We do not see the things that other participants are doing as completely disconnected from us. If I am in an orchestra and other members do their parts, they contribute to something that I care about as a final end. And when I do my part, I contribute to something that they care about as a final end. Rather than being disconnected individuals, we are each absorbed into a larger social project that connects us to one another. This social connectedness then serves as a foundation for us to appreciate one another's talents, abilities and character traits.

Social union is one form of social connectedness. Another form is one that I will call *mutual affirmation*. Let's say that a person A 'stands with' a person B when A is oriented to form attitudes towards B's succeeding or failing in some subset of B's projects as if, in some attenuated sense, A were succeeding or failing in a subset of A's projects.

Two people are 'mutually affirming' when person A stands with person B and person B stands with person A.[1] When two people stand with each other in this way, they affirm each other's importance and share in each other's fate.

Many normative relationships demand that those who stand in these relationships should be mutually affirming in some way. The most obvious case is friendship. If you and I are friends, then friendship demands that when I think about the possibility of your succeeding in certain projects that are important to you, I should regard this as something to hope for, and if you actually succeed, I should be happy about it.[2] Similarly, when I think about the possibility of your failing in certain projects that are important to you, I should regard this as something to be anxious about, and if you actually fail, that I should be disheartened. The relationship makes similar demands on you with respect to me.

Many normative relationships demand some form of mutual affirmation. The most important example, for my purposes, is the *political relationship*. Many philosophers believe that the members of a political community stand in a social relationship that has some features in common with friendship. The political relationship makes demands not only on how people act, but also on the attitudes that they form. As members of a political community, citizens should be mutually affirming in the sense that each citizen should form attitudes towards some subset of the successes and failures of her fellow citizens as if she were (in some attenuated sense) succeeding or failing in a corresponding subset of her own projects. We can think of the relevant subset in terms of a conception of the *common good*. This conception may take the form of a list of abstract goods that any citizen has reason to secure as part of a framework for realising her more particular objectives: these goods include things such as income, wealth, health care and a public basis for self-respect. On the 'common good' interpretation, the political relationship demands a kind of solidarity among citizens. For example, the relationship demands that each citizen should hope that her fellow citizens secure a sound public basis for self-respect and that she should be happy if her fellow citizens secure such a basis. And each citizen should be anxious about her fellow citizens failing to secure a sound public basis for self-respect and be disheartened if this failure ever becomes a reality.

Social union and mutual affirmation articulate different conceptions of social connectedness. At the heart of social union is the idea of a *cooperative activity*. In social union, the connection between people is 'external' in the sense that each person's connection to the others runs through a group activity which they each value: the activity is what each person contributes to and what each person cares about. In an orchestra, for instance, what ties the members of the orchestra to one another is the fact that each player finds that the actions of the others contribute to something that she cares about as a final end, namely playing beautiful orchestral music.

With mutual affirmation, on the other hand, the central idea is *solidarity*. In mutual affirmation, the connection between people is 'internal' in the sense that it involves each citizen thinking and acting in ways that accord a certain status to the good of other citizens. In the political relationship, for example, what ties members of the political community together is that each citizen is prepared to treat some of the ups and downs in her fellow citizens' lives as she were going through something similar. Social connectedness in this case is closely connected with caring and empathy (Figures 1 and 2).

Political philosophers often fail to distinguish clearly between cooperation and solidarity. This is in part because the distinction between self-interested behaviour and 'pro-social' behaviour is so important in modern economics that the differences between various forms of 'pro-social' behaviour tend to fall out of the picture. I will not pursue these issues further here since it would take us too far afield. I am interested in developing a particular kind of argument against competitive social institutions based on the idea of mutual affirmation. I offer the contrast with social union mainly as a way of clarifying the relevant form of connectedness.

Mutual affirmation and competitive institutions

Mutual affirmation represents one way of thinking about social connectedness. From now on my discussion will focus on this idea. For the purposes of my

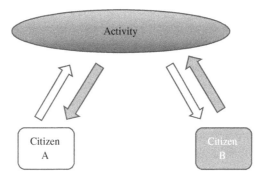

Figure 1. Social union.
Notes: In Rawls's conception of social union, people are connected through a group activity. Citizen A does her part in the shared plan, and B recognises A's activities as contributing to something that B cares about as a final end. Citizen B does her part in the shared plan, and A recognises B's activities as contributing to something that B cares about as a final end.

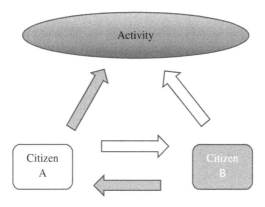

Figure 2. Mutual affirmation.
Notes: In mutual affirmation, each citizen is directly connected to her fellow citizens. A 'stands with' B, so she forms attitudes as if some subset of B's projects were A's projects as well. B 'stands with' A, so she forms attitudes as if some subset of A's projects were B's projects as well.

argument, it is important to see that some social institutions are more consistent with certain forms of mutual affirmation and others are less so.

Let me explain what I mean when I say that some social institutions are 'more consistent' with a certain form of mutual affirmation and others 'less so.' As I understand it, mutual affirmation is not primarily a physical state or a physical process. Mutual affirmation is best understood as a set of normative demands: it is a pattern of activity to which people may conform or fail to conform. For example, friendship demands a certain form of mutual affirmation: each of the individuals who stands in the relationship should think and act in certain ways, actively forming certain attitudes in response to the possibility of the other person's succeeding or failing in certain projects.

An institution is 'more consistent' with a certain form of mutual affirmation when it creates fewer and less serious obstacles to people thinking and acting in the ways that the relationship requires. An institution is 'less consistent' with a certain form of mutual affirmation when it creates more and more serious obstacles to people thinking and acting in the relevant ways. Consistency here is a measure of the extent to which the institution's design is consistent with a commitment to living up to the requirements of a certain form of mutual affirmation.

Consider now the case of a competitive arrangement. Baseball, for instance, is a competitive enterprise. The rules of the game define a certain status, i.e. 'winning' and they define a certain process for achieving this status. Each team has good reason to pursue the valuable status, but the activity is structured in such a way that the only way for members of one team to achieve the status is by preventing members of the other team from doing so. If team A gets a run, thereby taking one step closer to winning, this necessarily amounts to a setback for team B – that's one more run that team B needs in order to win. The same holds true when team B gets a run: this constitutes a setback for team A. The institution puts each team in a situation where members must effectively damage the project of the other team as a necessary side effect of the pursuit of their own aims.

Recall that people are mutually affirming when person A forms attitudes towards some subset of B's projects as if these were also, in some attenuated sense, A's projects (and vice versa). Suppose that the two teams in a baseball game are playing for an important prize: members of the winning team will get scholarships to a good university. None of the players could afford to go to college without these scholarships. But now suppose that all of the players – players on both teams – also stand in a certain social relationship with one another. For instance, suppose that the players are also all members of the same extended family or members of the same high-school community. Suppose further that the social relationship that binds them all demands a certain form of mutual affirmation. For example, membership in a family requires family members to share in one another's college aspirations or membership in a high school community requires classmates to share in one another's college aspirations.

The competitive structure of the game clearly creates significant obstacles to the players being mutually affirming in the way that the wider relationship requires. Given the competitive structure of the baseball game, a step forward for the members of one team constitutes a step backward for the members of the other. If team A scores a run, this will necessarily push the members of team B further from getting the college scholarships – that's one more run they need to make up. But the only way for the members of team A to get the scholarships is to score runs and win the game. So, in effect, the only way for the members of team A to reach their objective is by demolishing the aspirations of the team B. With every run team A scores, they are destroying the college aspirations of the members of team B. Team A could not do this effectively if members were also, at the same time, sharing in the failures of team B. As such, the structure of the competitive enterprise gives the members of team A powerful reasons to 'distance' themselves from the members of team B, that is, not to form attitudes towards the failures of team B in the way that is required by the wider social relationship. The same thing plays out from team B's perspective with regard to team A.

The point of the example is to draw attention to the tension between the structure of a competitive institution and the solidarity that is required by more encompassing relationships. The competitive structure of the baseball game creates significant reasons for the members of each team to 'distance' themselves from the members of the other team. As some might put it, the game sets the stage for 'man's alienation from his fellow man.'

I want to stress that the moral status of a competitive institution does not depend simply on its competitive structure, but also on the stakes involved. Ordinary moral thinking recognises the idea of a 'friendly competition.' An institution falls into this category when it has a competitive structure that generates reasons for distancing, but the reasons are not antithetical to the relevant form of mutual affirmation. There are two significant possibilities: (1) the reasons for distancing may not bear on the attitudes that matter in the relationship or (2) the reasons for distancing may be relatively minor. Consider again the case of a baseball game among the members of a family or a school community. Suppose that, instead of college scholarships, the winners simply get a beer at the losers' expense. Here, the competitive structure of the game gives players on each team reasons to distance themselves from the players on the other team. But (1) these are not reasons for distancing with respect to one another's college aspirations and (2) these reasons are not very serious. Since the reasons for distancing lack relevance and urgency, the institution is not antithetical to the relevant form of mutual affirmation – it is a friendly competition.[3]

A final point of clarification. Some readers might assume that any institution that distributes scarce goods must be competitive. But, as I understand it, the competitive character of an institution is never simply a function of background facts about scarcity. Suppose that there are 100 people in a community who need a kidney transplant and there are only 10 available kidneys. There is nothing the community can do to reduce the need for kidneys or to increase the supply. In the face of an absolute shortage, one thing the community could do is distribute kidneys by means of a lottery: under a lottery scheme, the kidney transplants would go to 10 patients drawn from the 100 at random. Of course, there are various reasons that might tell against a lottery scheme in this case. But the important point for my purposes is that under the lottery scheme, there is no way for any of the patients to formulate and carry out a plan that would undermine the prospects of any other patient. The institution does not put patients in a position where they can damage one another's prospects for getting a kidney,

Public goods and the sphere of competition

At this point, I want to make the discussion more concrete by relating the moral status of competitive institutions to certain questions about public policy. Imagine for the moment that a liberal democratic society is considering a set of measures to weaken its public health care system. As it stands, citizens receive medical coverage, independently of their ability to pay, and the community collectively bears the costs of providing health care to each individual. The proposal is to change the system so that individual citizens will have to enter the labour market to secure a market wage and then buy medical coverage for themselves and their dependents through a network of private insurers.

Let's assume that something short of full employment is the normal state of the economy. This means that there are at least some people who want a job and are actively looking for a job, but who cannot find a job. Short of full employment, the labour market is, at some level, a game of 'King of the Mountain': any one job hunter's formulating and successfully carrying out a plan to get a job will effectively block someone else in society from formulating and successfully carrying out a plan to get a job. A certain number of people can be in the workforce at any given time, and people get into the workforce and stay there by pushing other people out and keeping them out.

One thing that provisions for public goods do is they manage the stakes in labour market competition. When a society has a strong public health care system, one person's formulating and successfully carrying out a plan to get a job will have a limited impact on other people. A's success in getting a job will keep some other person B from getting a job, but this will typically deprive B only of the added income that comes with employment. But when society weakens its public health care system, this raises the stakes in labour market competition. A's success in getting a job will keep some other person B from getting a job, and the consequences for B are more severe: not only does this deprive B of the added income that comes from employment, but it also deprives B and B's dependents of health care.

Raising the stakes in labour market competition puts citizens on a different footing with one another. When a society weakens its public health care system, citizens find that they pose a more fundamental threat to one another. Any one citizens' obtaining health care for herself and her family requires that she take steps that will effectively prevent some other citizen from securing health care for herself and her family. Moreover, citizens are under constant pressure, as even those who have a job must constantly stay ahead of those who are looking for one in order to maintain their medical coverage. So when the stakes are higher, everyone has a more powerful reason to distance herself from the others. People must distance themselves from one another in order to effectively pursue something that matters more to each of them, i.e. medical coverage for themselves and their loved ones.

Of course, it may be acceptable for social institutions to pit citizens against each other to some degree: for example, it may be acceptable for institutions to pit people against each other with respect to moderate gains in income. But there is a limit: there is something morally objectionable about social institutions pitting people against each other with respect to extremely important goods, such as basic health care. As I noted at the outset, there is a difference between a friendly competition and a life or death struggle.[4] One of the strongest and most intuitive arguments for a public health care system is precisely that an arrangement of this kind is essential to avoid the situation where labour market competition descends into a struggle with life or death consequences.

The value of social connectedness (I): the instrumental view

How should we characterise the moral defect in competitive institutions that pit people against each other excessively? What exactly is wrong with a competitive labour market with potentially life or death consequences?

One account of the moral defect in excessively competitive institutions appeals to the instrumental value of social connectedness. Justice is a fundamental value and it requires people to act in certain ways towards one another. In order to act as justice requires, however, people must be adequately motivated to do so. According to the instrumental account, social connectedness plays an important role in generating an adequate motivation among citizens in a liberal democracy to treat one another as justice requires. On the instrumental account, the moral defect in excessively competitive institutions is that they are less likely to generate an adequate sense of justice in citizens.

Here is one way to flesh out the argument.

(A) Among other things, the principles of justice require citizens to offer just terms of social cooperation to their fellow citizens and to accept just terms of social cooperation when these are offered to them (see Rawls, 1999). More specifically, citizens in a liberal democracy must propose just laws in the public forum, whether as candidates, party officials or participants in public debates, and they must accept just laws when these are proposed by others.

(B) Reciprocity is a fundamental feature of human nature (Rawls, 1999, pp. 429–434; Rousseau, 1979). There is a basic psychological tendency in human beings such that when person A sees that person B acts with evident concern for A's good, then A will naturally form an attachment to B. The fact of reciprocity implies that an institution in which each participant's activity contributes to the good of others will naturally generate a richer network of social attachments than an institution in which each participant's activity detracts from the good of others.

(C) When A forms an attachment to B, A will be more powerfully moved by the justice or injustice of laws that affect B (Rawls, 1999, p. 426–427). So, other things being equal, when citizens are tied together in a dense network of social attachments, they are more likely to offer just terms of cooperation to one another and more likely to accept just terms when these are offered to them.

(D) In a competitive institution, participants have powerful reasons to act in ways that undermine one another's good. So, other things being equal, a competitive institution will generate a weaker and less dense network of social attachments. It follows that a society whose basic institutions are intensely competitive will generate a weaker and less dense network of social attachments and therefore a less powerful motivation in citizens to treat one another as justice requires.

To illustrate, consider again the case of a liberal democratic society that adopts a set of policies that weaken its public health care system. These policies raise the stakes in labour market competition. Under a more intensely competitive arrangement, each citizen finds that her fellow citizens are formulating and carrying out plans in the labour market that would effectively deprive her and her dependents of health care. Moreover, each citizen finds that she must formulate and carry out plans that would effectively deprive other citizens and their dependents of health care if she wants to secure health care for herself and her dependents. An institution of this kind leaves less room for citizens to act with evident concern for one another's good. As a result, the social order on the whole will generate a lower degree of mutual attachment among citizens and they will have a less powerful drive to offer just terms of social cooperation to others and to accept just terms when these are offered to them.

The instrumental account of the moral defect in competitive institutions has a great deal of plausibility. It appeals to widely observed facts about human nature and connects these facts with a fundamental value, i.e. social justice. One might supplement the basic argument I sketched above with a more complex view of the importance of social connectedness in moral development (e.g. Rawls, 1999, pp. 405–434) and the importance of social connectedness in each person's good (e.g. Rawls, 1999, pp. 456–464, 496–505). These elaborations would present a richer account of how competitive institutions might undermine the just character of a liberal democracy.

The problem with the instrumental account, as I understand it, is not that the account is false: I believe that the instrumental account is true and that excessively competitive institutions are morally defective in part because they impede the formation of a rich network of social attachments, which is necessary for maintaining just arrangements over time. The problem with the instrumental account is rather that, even if it is true, it cannot fully explain the moral defect in excessively competitive institutions. There are two main problems.

The first problem is that our judgements about the morally defective character of excessively competitive institutions are much more definitive than the empirical evidence would warrant. The instrumental account makes the moral status of competitive institutions depend on a series of empirical claims about (1) how people form attachments, (2) how these attachments develop under different institutional arrangements and (3) the role of these attachments in sustaining just institutions. The evidence for these claims is substantial, and a significant body of work in psychology, sociology and evolutionary biology supports them. But these claims represent one major paradigm of social explanation: there is another paradigm that explains the emergence and persistence of various social arrangements in terms of human dispositions that are oriented towards the rational pursuit of self-interest. To a significant degree, the same body of observations about society and social arrangements can be explained in terms of the 'rational choice' paradigm, and there is no particular reason to think that the evidence will ever come down definitively in favour of the reciprocity based view.

By contrast with the empirical evidence, however, our judgements about the moral defectiveness of institutions that pit people against each other excessively are quite definitive. We rightly recoil at the prospect of a labour market that is a life or death struggle. Since our judgements about these institutions are much more secure than the empirical case for a causal connection between competition and injustice would warrant, the instrumental account cannot be the whole story about the moral status of these institutions.

The second problem with the instrumental account has to do with the grounds of our judgements. When we judge a certain competitive institution to be defective because it pits people against each other excessively, we do so largely without regard for a causal connection between competition and injustice. To appreciate the point, it is important not to think about competitive institutions from the detached perspective of an economist or bureaucratic planner, but from the perspective of a participant. When I think about what life would be like in a labour market with life or death consequences, I have a strong sense of the immorality of the institution. As a competitor in the arrangement, I would resent being put in a position where I have to beat our other parents for jobs, effectively pushing their potentially sick children out of doctor's offices, in order to make sure that my children have access to medical care. My resentment would not focus primarily on the fact that, under this arrangement, I might not develop an adequate motivation to reject laws that treat other citizens unfairly and that other citizens might not develop an adequate motivation to reject laws that treat me unfairly. My resentment would focus primarily on the way that the arrangement shapes my interactions with my fellow citizens. The arrangement puts tremendous pressure on me to act in ways that express a kind of disregard for them (and their families) and it puts tremendous pressure on them to act in ways that express a kind of disregard for me (and my family). The arrangement throws us in a cage match, where the prize is so basic that we all have very little option but to do what it takes to win.

The immorality of institutions that pit people against each other excessively stems most directly from the way that these institutions require people to act with an extreme form of mutual disregard, a form that is inconsistent with ordinary notions of civility. It is this feature that grounds our moral judgements rather than the fact that these institutions may affect our motivation to act as justice requires in the political arena.

The value of social connectedness (II): the non-instrumental view

The instrumental account says that the moral defect in social institutions that pit people against each other excessively is that these arrangements will not generate the kind of social connectedness that is essential for citizens to develop an adequate sense of justice. I have shown how the instrumental account does not fit with the definitiveness of our judgements about excessively competitive institutions or with the grounds for our judgements. Is there another account of the moral defect in these arrangements that can supplement the instrumental account? I believe that there is.

The other account appeals to the *noninstrumental value* of social connectedness. Members of a political community stand in a political relationship with one another. Like friendship, this relationship requires a certain form of mutual affirmation among members. The disposition to be mutually affirming may be important for instrumental reasons, i.e. because it supports or 'complements' a sense of justice (see Cohen, 1997, 2010). But mutual affirmation is intrinsically important because it is a requirement of the political relationship. Insofar as the political relationship requires a form of mutual affirmation among members, it also requires members to adopt institutions that are properly consistent with this activity. And the moral defect in excessively competitive institutions is that they are antithetical to the relevant form of mutual affirmation.

Here is one way to flesh out the argument.

(A) People born into a political community stand in a political relationship with one another (Dworkin, 1986; Marx, 1964; Rousseau, 1979). They are involved in a set of ongoing activities that transform the natural environment, socialise future generations, and articulate and enforce social institutions, thereby reproducing the community over time. Taking part in these activities gives rise to what Dworkin calls 'associative obligations': in much the way that involvement in shared activities and a shared history gives rise to obligations among the members of a family, involvement in shared activities and a shared history gives rise to obligation among the members of a political community (compare Kolodny, 2010).

(B) Mutual affirmation focused on a conception of the common good is a requirement of the political relationship (Rousseau, 1979, 1997a, 1997b). The relationship requires citizens to be oriented to share in the successes and failures of their fellow citizens with respect to securing income, wealth, health care and a public basis for self-respect.

(C) If a relationship requires that people should be mutually affirming with respect to certain projects, then the relationship also requires that people should adopt institutions and practices that are consistent with these forms of mutual affirmation. For example, if the marriage relationship requires partners to share in one another's successes and failures with respect to their careers, then the relationship also requires partners to adopt marriage practices that are properly consistent with this form of solidarity – i.e. the relationship does not allow partners to adopt practices that give them powerful reasons to undermine one another's careers.

(D) The political relationship requires citizens to be mutually affirming with respect to securing elements of the common good. It follows that the relationship prohibits citizens from adopting institutions that give them powerful reasons to distance themselves from one another with respect to these projects. Excessively competitive institutions create significant reasons for distancing of this kind so the political relationship prohibits members from adopting these types of arrangements.

To illustrate, consider again a set of policies that would weaken a public health care system. In a market society, these policies would lead to labour market competition with potentially life or death consequences. From the standpoint of the instrumental account, the moral defect in a labour market of this kind is that the social order would not generate an appropriate motivation in citizens to treat one another as justice requires. But from the standpoint of the noninstrumental account, the moral defect does not stem from a causal connection between competition and injustice.

From the standpoint of the noninstrumental account, the moral defect in a labour market with life or death consequences stems from the requirements of the wider political relationship. The relationship that binds members of a political community together requires that they should be mutually affirming with respect to the projects that constitute the common good. The community is properly understood as a group whose members must stand in solidarity with one another, not unlike a group of friends or neighbours, as they work together to secure certain achievements for each member. Let's say that securing health care for oneself and one's dependents is among the projects that make up the common good. Given that health care is among these projects, the political relationship requires that members should adopt institutions that not only secure health care for members, but also do not put members in circumstances where they have powerful reasons to undermine one another with respect to their health care coverage.

Notice that the noninstrumental account fits better with the two features of our judgements about excessively competitive institutions that I mentioned earlier. First, our moral judgements about excessively competitive institutions are quite definitive, but the empirical evidence about the relationship between competition and injustice is not. According to the noninstrumental account, the moral defect in excessively competitive institution does not depend on any causal connection between competition and injustice, so the fact that the empirical evidence for this connection is ambiguous does not bear on our judgements about the moral defectiveness of these arrangements.

Second, our judgements about excessively competitive institutions are not grounded primarily in the impact that these institutions may have on legislative motivations. According to the noninstrumental account, the moral defect in excessively competitive institutions does not have to do with the fact that these institutions may not generate an adequate motivation in citizens to treat one another appropriately in political rule-making. Instead, the moral defect in these arrangements has to do with the reasons that these institutions create for citizens to act with a kind of disregard for one another in the civil sphere. This fits better with the intuitive grounds for our judgements.

Some might object to the noninstrumental account because it appeals to a demanding view of the political relationship. According to the noninstrumental account, the political relationship has a feature in common with friendship, as it requires citizens not only to act in certain ways, but also to form certain attitudes and to reason in certain ways. This may seem excessively demanding. In response, I would stress that the political relationship is not necessarily a standard for assessing the conduct of individual citizens. For the purposes of my argument, the political relationship is rather an ideal of social interaction, an ideal that serves as part of a standard for assessing *social institutions*. The theoretical objective is to formulate a conception of proper interaction among citizens that can then account for our judgements about the moral defect in certain social institutions, such as a labour market with life or death consequences. The concept of a political relationship can serve as part of a conception of properly ordered institutions, even if it does not also provide a standard for assessing individual conduct.

Conclusion

A certain degree of competition in social life is clearly acceptable, but – just as clearly – there are limits: social institutions can be morally defective when they pit people against each other excessively. Over the course of this paper, I have developed a particular way of thinking about the moral defect in these institutions. Excessively competitive institutions are antisocial and antithetical to certain forms of social connectedness. The value of social connectedness is not primarily instrumental: the problem with a life or death labour market is not simply that it interferes with the kind of connectedness that helps to maintain just arrangements over time. The value of social connectedness is also noninstrumental: excessively competitive institutions are morally defective because they are inconsistent with the kind of mutual affirmation that is required by the political relationship. So the full story about the moral defect in excessively competitive institutions has two parts: (a) arrangements of this kind are less likely to generate the kind of social connectedness that is necessary for an adequate sense of justice and (b) arrangements of this kind directly violate the solidaristic requirements of the political relationship.

Notes

1. A 'stands with' B when A is *oriented* to form certain attitudes towards the possibility of B's succeeding or failing. This means that A will form the relevant attitudes when the relevant facts come to A's attention. In most cases, people in a relationship are not constantly in each other's presence, so what the relationship requires is an orientation to form certain attitudes. The relationship may also require people to gather certain forms of information and monitor others' progress, and it may require them to give each other space.
2. There are, of course, limits. If you are a paedophile, for example, then I have no reason to share in your happiness about your success in this project.
3. Even Rousseau (1960, pp. 126, 127, 1979, p. 352, 1997b, p. 191) gives games and competitions a place in the ideal republic.
4. There are important questions to consider here about when exactly the stakes in a competitive institution become excessive. But for my purposes in this paper, I will set these questions aside and use the case of a labour market with life and death consequences as a relatively clear example of an arrangement that crosses the line.

Disclosure statement

No potential conflict of interest was reported by the author.

References

Cohen, J. (1997). The natural goodness of humanity. In A. Reath, B. Herman, & C. M. Korsgaard (Eds.), *Reclaiming the history of ethics: Essays for John Rawls* (pp. 102–149). Cambridge: Cambridge University Press.

Cohen, J. (2010). *Rousseau: A free community of equals.* Oxford: Oxford University Press.

Dworkin, R. (1986). *Law's empire.* Cambridge: Harvard University Press.

Kolodny, N. (2010). Which relationships justify partiality? The case of parents and children. *Philosophy & Public Affairs, 38*(1), 37–75.

Marx, K. (1964). *The economic and philosophical manuscripts of 1844.* (M. Milligan, Trans.). New York, NY: International Publishers.

Rawls, J. (1999). *A theory of justice* (revised ed.). Cambridge: Harvard University Press.

Rousseau, J. (1960). Letter to M. D'Alembert on the theatre. In *Politics and the arts.* (A. Bloom, Trans.). Ithaca, NY: Cornell University Press.

Rousseau, J. (1979). *Emile.* A. Bloom (Ed.). New York, NY: Basic Books.

Rousseau, J. (1997a). On the social contract. In V. Gourevitch (Ed.), *The social contract and later political writings* (pp. 39–152). Cambridge: Cambridge University Press.

Rousseau, J. (1997b). Considerations on the government of Poland. In V. Gourevitch (Ed.), *The social contract and later political writings* (pp. 177–260). Cambridge: Cambridge University Press.

Racial structural solidarity

Mara Marin

ABSTRACT

Effective political action against racial injustice requires a conception of solidarity based on the social and material reality of this form of injustice. I develop such a notion of solidarity by extending Iris Young's notion of 'gender as seriality' to race. This notion of solidarity avoids the problems encountered by Shelby's 'common oppression view' and Gooding-Williams's non-foundational view. On Shelby's 'common oppression' view, solidarity is based solely on the victims' shared condition of oppression. According to Shelby, all victims of racial oppression can be reasonably expected to endorse a set of principles that will move them to common action. Gooding-Williams sheds doubt on the idea that such shared principles exist and defends instead a view of politics as action-in-concert, marked by reasonable disagreement, and a non-foundational view of solidarity constituted through the controversy of politics rather than given in virtue of pre-political commitments or interests. I argue that the problem with such a notion is that it is unable to link the material and social reality of the unjust structures to the forms of political action that would effectively transform social reality. My notion of 'structural racial solidarity' would avoid these problems.

In the recent primary elections for the Democratic Party nominee for president of the USA, Ta-Nehisi Coates, a journalist for *The Atlantic*, sparked a debate about the black vote when he criticized Sanders for not supporting reparations.[1] This refusal, Coates thinks, proves Sanders to have a typically 'class first' race-blind socialist program that fails to appreciate that addressing issues of minimum wage and poverty does not address issues of white supremacy, such as discrimination in the labor market or under the law.

A number of African-American intellectuals[2] have criticized Coates's criticism of Sanders as indicative of an approach that separates racial from class oppression and rests, in the words of Cedric Johnson, on a claim of 'racial parity' within a capitalist, market society that leaves untouched the deeper sources of inequality and poverty that lie in the overarching processes of capitalist accumulation and the commodification of human needs.[3]

This debate raises the question of anti-racist solidarity: How should we conceive of solidarity for an effective anti-racist politics?

I turn to Tommie Shelby's and Robert Gooding-Williams's works on black solidarity to tackle this question. I argue that, their differences notwithstanding, they share a view of political action that identifies the unity of collective political action with the political purposes deliberately shared by political actors, thus failing to theorize the relationship between political action and the social and material reality it aims to change. This is a shortcoming for an account of solidarity for effective anti-racist politics for two reasons. First, because such an account needs to offer a picture of the changes aimed at by the collective effort. Second, because it needs to offer an account of the sources of the actors' power to affect those changes. We need a structural understanding of race, one that I sketch by extending Iris Young's conception of 'gender as seriality' to race.

Shelby on black solidarity as common oppression

'In an effort to liberate blacks from the burden of racial oppression, black leaders have frequently called on black Americans to become a more unified collective agent for social change' (Shelby, 2002, p. 231). Thus, Shelby defines the problem of solidarity as that of forging a unified collective agent out of the individuals burdened by racial oppression, a collective agent that acts to change the reality of racial oppression. For Shelby, solidarity is about the motivation for action. It has to be 'robust' enough 'to move people to collective action' (Shelby, 2002, p. 237).

For Shelby, the question of solidarity is the question of its foundation. There are five characteristics necessary and jointly sufficient for solidarity: identification with the group, special concern for the group's other members, shared values or goals, group loyalty and mutual trust (Shelby, 2005, pp. 68–70). He rejects 'the collective identity theory' that holds that 'blacks who are committed to emancipatory group solidarity must embrace and preserve their distinctive black identity' (Shelby, 2002, p. 233) by arguing that such identity is not necessary for satisfying these conditions and may be self-defeating (Shelby, 2002, p. 235). In contrast, black solidarity should be based on the shared condition of being a victim of antiblack racism, because the common experience of being a victim of antiblack racism provides sufficient basis for the five characteristics of solidarity (Shelby, 2002, pp. 247, 248).

What is 'antiblack racism' and who are its victims? For Shelby (2005), racism is an ideology, 'a set of misleading and irrationally held beliefs and assumptions,' such as the belief that blacks are intellectually inferior, 'that serve to bring about and reinforce structural relations of oppression' and that 'are socially reproduced through norms that are embedded in the culture.' Such irrational beliefs are held because of often unacknowledged fears and desires, such as the white working class fear about unemployment and competition over scarce jobs. Racism – explicit or implicit – continues to be expressed by many (p. 142).

Understood in this way, antiblack racism is only one among three sources of black disadvantage. The other two are (1) the effects of past racial domination, which create disadvantages for *some* blacks and (2) non-racial structural factors that have a negative impact on the life prospects of *some* blacks (Shelby, 2005, pp. 141–144).

The first of these two, disadvantages that can be traced to past racial domination, are the effects in the present of chattel slavery, land expropriation, segregation, etc. Racial disparities in wealth and education, for instance, can be traced to the history of discrimination as a result of which generations of black Americans were prevented from accumulating wealth and gaining a formal education.

The second, 'non-racial structural factors' are created by social dynamics that cannot be attributed to racism, for instance the

> Postindustrial US economy that generally dispenses high rewards to persons with a college education and miserably low wages to those without; stagnation and decline in economic sectors that rely heavily on low-skilled workers; and changes in the tax code that favor individuals and households with significant financial assets. None of these developments rely directly on contemporary expressions of racism to produce their far-reaching social consequences. Yet they disproportionately impact blacks in a society where deep racial inequalities in education, employment opportunities, and wealth already exist, and they worsen racial inequality and create new forms of disadvantage. (Shelby, 2005, pp. 143, 144)

For example, the tax benefits that flow from homeownership are not racist in Shelby's terms, because they are not necessarily designed to discriminate against blacks, but they disproportionately disadvantage blacks, because they are less likely to own a home, or more likely to own a less expensive home (Shelby, 2005, p. 144).

Among these three sources of black disadvantage, Shelby argues, *only* racism qualifies as the basis of black solidarity because it is the only one that can unite *all* black Americans and can secure their commitment to fight together, for only the ideology that thinly black persons are inferior affects all black persons.

Shelby (2005) develops this argument by translating the question of solidarity into a Rawls-an sounding question: 'What political principles can blacks reasonably expect *all* other black, because they are black, to commit to as a basis for group action?' (p. 155).

In determining these principles, i.e. principles that blacks can *reasonably* expect *all* other blacks to commit to, just in virtue of their being black, Shelby argues that the differences among black Americans can threaten black solidarity. Therefore, support for policies that 'disproportionately impact' black Americans is not a reliable basis for political unity. *Black* solidarity requires collective action around consensus issues, and racism is the only such issue (pp. 155, 160).[4]

SOLIDARITY AND PUBLIC GOODS

I want to raise two problems with this view.

A first problem is that it reduces solidary action to self-interested action. Shelby assumes that the likelihood that some people will defect from those forms of collective action that do not advance their interest is a reason to restrict the scope of black politics to those issues that affect the interests of *all* black people. But if shared interest can motivate us – as Shelby's argument assumes – we do not need solidarity, for we can rely on the shared interest to do so. Solidarity, one might have thought, is necessary precisely where and because self-interest fails to motivate action. There is something unsatisfying about a view of solidarity that can deliver nothing more than what self-interest can.

A second problem, which Robert Gooding-Williams (2009, pp. 230–234) and Lawrie Balfour (2006) have pointed out, is that racism is not a unified phenomenon. Drawing on Cathy Cohen's distinction between consensus and cross-cutting issues of black activism, they have argued that different groups of black people are affected by different sets of stereotypes and different forms of discrimination. Black feminists, among others, have argued that the antiblack racism's representations of black women – as mammy, matriarch, jezebel, welfare queen, etc. – apply specifically to black women, and they are intrinsically gendered, not particular instances of generic, antiblack stereotypes. Therefore, there is no shared interest in supporting collective action against a putatively generic antiblack racism, as such action will likely only further marginalize the cross-cutting issues that reflect minority interests.

If this is right, then we need to revisit the privileged place Shelby gives racism in his understanding of racial disadvantage. Recall that Shelby distinguishes between three sources of black disadvantage and argues that two of them – the effects of past racial discrimination and social dynamics that cannot be attributed to racism – are not properly the object of *black* politics. Let's take the latter, policies that disproportionately affect black Americans, such as IRS-mandated benefits that flow to home ownership, and accept that they are not motivated by racism, but are created by social dynamics and policies that give advantages to wealth, and larger advantages to larger wealth. Shelby (2005, pp. 149, 153, 154) argues that although these social dynamics disproportionately affect black Americans, they are not proper targets of anti-racist action, because they do not affect *all* black Americans, but only the poorer ones. This shows, Shelby thinks, that black Americans are disproportionately affected by policies that give advantage to wealth because they are disproportionately among the less wealthy, not because they are black. Such policies should be the target of a different type of politics – a politics that targets wealth inequality, which any black person could join – but not of specifically black politics.

Let me analyze this argument through an analogy with policies that disproportionately affect women. On this reasoning, the lack of affordable, good-quality childcare that disproportionately affects women is not a proper target of feminist action because it does not affect all women, but only those who are primary childcare providers. This disproportionate impact is due to the fact that women happen to be disproportionately represented among the (separately constituted) group of primary childcare providers, i.e. mothers, not because they are women. Hence, unless motivated by sexism, the lack of childcare facilities is not a proper target of feminist politics.

There is indeed a good case to be made that the lack of childcare facilities affects women even when it is not motivated by sexism. It does so in virtue of its intersection with other social practices, processes and structures, such as the modern organization of work as separate from care, and the lower value placed on the latter. However, feminists widely agree that the disadvantages flowing from the lack of childcare facilities are central to the disadvantages that women experience in virtue of their gender, and thus to the mechanisms that reproduce gender oppression, whether or not sexism has anything to do with it. If sexism has nothing to do with the lack of childcare facilities, then sexism is not a good explanation for these mechanisms. It does not mean that these mechanisms are not gendered in another sense. To insist that sexism alone should be the target of feminist politics because it alone affects all women is to prejudge this question of the best explanation for gender disadvantage, to assume what has to be shown.

Shelby makes a similar mistake in privileging racism as the sole object of black politics: he prejudges the issue of the best explanation of racial disadvantage and the mechanisms that reproduce it. A policy that disproportionately affects black Americans requires an explanation. To say by way of explanation that black Americans are disproportionately among the less wealthy, and *therefore the disproportionate effect is not a matter of their race, but of their wealth level*, is to assume that race and wealth level are independent factors.

This explanation is similar to saying that women are disproportionately affected by the lack of childcare facilities only because they are disproportionately among mothers, not because they are women, thus assuming that 'women' and 'mothers' have entirely independent meanings and represent groups constituted through independent social practices. This is an assumption challenged by every feminist analysis of the connections between the social meanings of 'woman' and 'mother,' and between the social practices that constitute the two groups. That there are such connections does not mean that we cannot conceive of a woman who is not a mother, but that all women are subject to norms that include expectations about their role as mothers.

Similarly, racial and wealth disadvantage might very well be connected in the sense that the social practices that constitute race are connected to those that structure the creation and accumulation of wealth. There is no reason to assume, as Shelby does, that the two are independent. On the contrary, that black Americans are disproportionately among the less wealthy is a reason to think the opposite, that one's race is connected to one's ability to acquire wealth. Moreover, the connections between the American practices of race and slavery and segregation also suggest such a connection, given the economic impact of slavery and segregation on one's access to wealth.

We need therefore a conception of race that enables us to ask questions about these connections. This is a conception of race that does not reduce race to either the practice of assigning individuals to different racial groups, or to the ideological set of beliefs underpinning this practice, but connects it to the social and material processes that support and perpetuate it.

Gooding-Williams on non-foundational solidarity

By building on feminist conceptions of intersectionality, Gooding-Williams's argument that different groups of black Americans are affected by different forms of racism might be a more promising point of departure for such a conception of race.

As an alternative to Shelby's common oppression view of solidarity, Gooding-Williams (2009) suggests a non-foundational idea of solidarity that is forged in action (p. 238) rather than being based on something that precedes politics. This type of solidarity requires the reinvigoration of different publics of black politics (pp. 241, 242).

This view of black politics is informed by Gooding-Williams's reading of Douglass's thought in *Bondage*, according to which Douglass proposes a notion of politics as a practice of 'action in concert' between equals. Politics, on this view, is a practice of freedom based on consent and affiliation opposed to the kinship ties that slavery denies to slaves. In Douglass's thought, the plantation version of this politics is represented by the 'band of brothers' that, having been thrown together on Mr. Freeland's plantation, begin to consult one another, to debate and deliberate the merits of different courses of action, thus cultivating ties of loyalty, and forming themselves 'into a band of subversive activists' by 'consenting through their speech, action and mutual commitments to resist slaveholder tyranny.' In this way, they form 'affiliative relationships to one another – that is, *because each has agreed to adopt as his own* a mutually shaped sense of political purpose.' In short, according to Gooding-Williams (2009), 'Douglass portrays plantation politics as an enterprise of equals driven by a shared and discursively expressed concern to free the world of "tyrants and oppressors"' (pp. 186, 187, emphasis added).

Understood in this way, politics can and sometimes should be race-conscious, but in being so it need not be based on 'antecedently formed and racially specific spiritual or cultural orientation.' Gooding-Williams agrees here with Shelby in rejecting the collective identity theory. But, unlike Shelby, he thinks the race dimension is created through politics rather than being pre-political. It is created discursively by political actors, produced through a process in which political actors invest with significance the condition of being black in light of their interpretation of what their political purposes demand (Gooding-Williams, 2009, pp. 189, 190).

This harkens back to Gooding-Williams's (1998) earlier distinction between 'being black' and 'being a black person.' 'Being black' is 'the product of a rule-governed social practice of racial classification,' while 'being a black person' is the result of one's 'interpreting and assigning significance to being black' (pp. 22, 24). While one cannot escape being black, one is thrown into the condition of being black by a racist social practice, being a black person is a matter of self-description, of assigning meaning to that condition. Thus, one 'becomes a black person only if (1) one begins to identify ... *oneself* as black and (2) one begins to make choices, to formulate plans, to express concerns, etc., in light of one's identification of oneself as black' (p. 23) Gooding-Williams points to Sartre's notion of being a Jew, according to which to be a Jew 'is to be thrown into ... the situation of a Jew' (Sartre, 1995, p. 89; cited in Gooding-Williams, 1998, p. 25) as similar to his notion of being black. In explaining the notion of being a black person, he draws on Ian Hacking's notion of 'dynamic nominalism' and its underlying thought that the possibilities of human action depend on the possibilities of description, such that 'if new modes of description come into being, new possibilities of action come into being in consequence' (Hacking, 1986, p. 231; cited in Gooding-Williams, 1998, p. 23). Thus, 'individuals classified as black become black persons just in case they begin to act in the world under a description of themselves as racially black' (p. 23).

This means that there are many ways of being a black person, corresponding to the many and conflicting interpretations of being black (Gooding-Williams, 1998, p. 24, 2009, p. 191), including interpretations that embrace the racial order as just (Gooding-Williams, 2009, p. 190). This diversity is at the heart of Gooding-Williams's (2009, p. 239) view of black politics 'as the interplay of conflicting purposes with conflicting and likely controversial interpretations of the condition of being black,' a non-foundational model of politics that he contrasts to Shelby's. A crucial difference between Shelby's model of politics and his own, Gooding-Williams (2009, p. 238) argues, is that the former conceives of 'common black interests' as given prior to politics, as something that political participants 'precommit' themselves to, while on his model common black interests might come out of politics itself, as the result of political argument, debate or collective action, for instance when the participants try to persuade each other of one particular interpretation of the condition of being black, including one account of the common interests that the condition entails.

While an attractive alternative to Shelby's, this picture of politics as marked by deep disagreement runs into its own problems. First, it is in tension with the 'action-in-concert' aspect of politics that Gooding-Williams (2009) also emphasizes. Douglass's the band of brothers acts in concert because they agree to resist slaveholder tyranny. They form affiliative relationships to one another because 'each has agreed to adopt as his own a mutually shaped sense of political purpose'. It is true that these affiliative, consent-based relationships may be formed as part of politics – consent is expressed 'through their speech, actions and mutual commitments' – yet to the degree to which they act in concert they already share a purpose – 'to resist slaveholder tyranny' (p. 186). So while there is a non-foundational aspect to their politics, to the degree to which they arrive at common purposes through politics, there is another aspect, the action aspect, of their politics that is not. For they act-in-concert only once these purposes are taken as given. Thus, Douglass's band of brothers could not be said to act-in-concert with those who have fallen prey to 'the slaveholding priestcraft,' the view that slavery is God's will. The two groups could engage in debate and argument, each group trying to persuade the other to adopt their interpretation of the condition of being black, but they could not act together. This shows that the acting-in-concert aspect of politics requires agreement around common purposes even though politics has a deliberative aspect, one that is marked by deep disagreement. In other words, to the degree to which politics is action, not only debate and argument, Gooding-Williams's view of politics is not crucially different from Shelby's. Those who act together do so based on an agreed-upon common purpose; there may be room for disagreement on the details of this purpose, and on the means to achieve it, but there is no reason to believe that such disagreement is blocked on Shelby's account. In its action aspect, politics, even for Gooding-Williams, is unified by shared purposes. Acting-in-concert, is acting-for-shared-purposes.

It is important to note that the act through which these purposes are adopted is fundamentally an individual, not a political one. Adopting particular purposes is part of one's process of 'becoming a black person,' of assigning meaning and significance to the condition of being black. There is nothing essentially political about this act. It could take place in public, it could be spurred by political encounters – encounters with other political actors – but it could equally take place in private, independently of political encounters. Even when the act is spurred by political engagement, and even if political engagement were necessary to it, politics would still be externally related to it, not a constitutive condition, because, on Gooding-Williams's account of it, it represents the interpretation taken by an individual, and over which the individual is more or less sovereign.

If this interpretation is right, it sheds more doubts on Gooding-Williams's claim that his view of politics is non-foundational. For it suggests that there is a non-political act that precedes and is necessary for political action.

Furthermore, it raises another difficulty for Gooding-Williams's view of political action. In defining the 'in-concert' character of the political action by reference to shared purposes, adopted deliberately, Gooding-Williams's view of politics as action-in-concert leaves behind the social and material reality that forms the background against which such purposes are chosen and pursued in the world. By relying on Hacking's view that human action depends on description, a view according to which description is an individual act of meaning-making, of creating something *new* in the world, Gooding-Williams's view of politics as action-in-concert obscures the fact that the possibilities of action depend not only on new descriptions, but also on the material and social reality that is already in place. It obscures the fact that the possibilities for political action and what makes it effective depend not only on the purposes of the actors, but also on the social and material conditions within which action takes place. By making conceptual sense of the process of 'becoming a black person' in terms of the Hacking's 'dynamic nominalism,' and connecting this process conceptually to the notion of 'action-in-concert,' Gooding-Williams throws away, and therefore partly obscures, the throwness character of the condition of being black.

My criticism of Shelby's and Gooding-Williams's positions in the last two sections suggests that we need a conception of race that would achieve two tasks. First, it would have to provide an understanding of the social reality of racial disadvantage that would make sense of the unity of racial disadvantage while also enabling inquiry into its connections to social processes that create disadvantages for groups other than black Americans. By doing this, it would also avoid the problems associated with denying differences in how race and racial disadvantage is experienced by different groups of black Americans. Second, it would have to provide a notion of action that links political action to the social reality of racial disadvantage. In what follows I argue that Iris Young's concept of 'seriality' can be extended to the concept of race to provide such an understanding of race and racial disadvantage.

Young on seriality and gender as seriality

Iris Young (1997) borrows Sartre's concept of seriality to articulate an understanding of gender that, she argues, represents an understanding of women as a unified group that does not deny differences among women (pp. 17, 22).

Sartre distinguishes between several levels of social collectivity by their complexity and reflexivity. One of the distinctions he makes is that between groups and series. A group is a self-consciously mutually acknowledging collective with a self-conscious purpose. It is a collection of persons that are united by the action they undertake together. Individuals undertake a project together and acknowledge themselves as sharing a set of goals and as pursuing these goals through their actions. Each individual takes on the common project as his or her project. 'What makes the project *shared* ... is the mutual acknowledgement among the members of the group that they are engaged in the project together,' which typically becomes explicit in something like 'a pledge, contract, constitution.' The project is *collective* in so far as the members of the group mutually acknowledge that the only or best way to undertake the project is by the group (Young, 1997, p. 23, emphasis added). For both Shelby and Gooding-Williams, I have argued above, political action is the action of such groups.

These self-conscious collectives arise from and often fall back into un-self-conscious collectives, which Sartre calls series. At this level of social reality, individuals are united, but not by shared goals and projects. They are united in an impersonal way, through particular constellations of material objects and structures or norms that constrain and enable their actions. What gives the individuals in a series *unity* is the way in which individuals pursue their own individual ends by reference to *the same* objects and structures that is the result, often unintended, of past actions.

Sartre illustrates the concept of a series with the example of people waiting for a bus. They are united by their relation to an object – the bus – and the social norms and practices that define that object as a bus, i.e. the social practice of public transportation. This constellation of objects, social norms and practices both constrains and enables their actions. Within these constraints, different individuals pursue different goals, aims and projects. From the point of view of their aims, the people in a series have nothing in common; they take different actions. However, they are united by their common orientation to the same objects and social practices. As part of the series, the individuals waiting for a bus need have nothing in common in their histories, experiences or identities. The relation between individuals in a series is impersonal and anonymous. Individuals are fungible; any individual could take any other individuals' place. They do not identify with one another; they do not acknowledge each other as engaged in a shared enterprise. The series is not a group, and its unity is not that of a group. However, the series has the potential to become a group. If the bus fails to show up, those who were waiting for it may complain to one another and may organize themselves to go protest the bus company or to share a taxi (p. 24).

The series is what Sartre calls a *practical-inert reality*. It is *practical* because it, like all social relations, is the result of human action and history. However, the type of action that creates a series is not a self-conscious one. Or, to be precise, the aspect of an action in virtue of which that action creates the series is not the conscious goal or purpose pursued by its agent. Rather, it is the action's unintended consequences and the action's relation to something external to the agents: the fact that their actions are constrained by the same norms and objects that are results of past action. Any material objects are experienced as *inert* because they constrain action and constitute resistance to action. This is why series, and being a member of a series, are experienced as necessities and constraints, often experienced as given and natural (p. 25).

More generally, on Sartre's view, any human action takes place against the background of the material things and collective habits, practices, rules, etc. that are the result of past human action oriented toward practical-inert objects in series, background that he calls 'the milieu of action.' Human action structured in this way – oriented toward and constrained by objects, and structured by practices, habits and rules that are already given – generate and continuously reproduce serial collectivities (p. 25).

Gender, Iris Young argues, should be understood as such a series. What recommends this understanding for her is that it makes sense of the idea that women form a social unity without casting that unity in terms of common attributes or essential features, which has the effect of erasing differences among women.

In addition, I would argue, Sartre's conception of human action as structured by practical-inert realities explains why social practices like gender and race are both resistant to change (because they are inert, i.e. reproduce themselves through action in the series) and can be changed (because they are practical, i.e. they are products of human action).

Gender is 'a structural relation to material objects as they have been produced and organized by prior history' (p. 28). But like 'class' and unlike 'bus riders,' 'gender' is a complex, vast, overlapping set of structures and objects. What are these objects and the structures that organize them?

Female bodies are among the objects in the series gender. Female bodies should be understood as social objects, not simply as material objects. It is not simply the physical attributes of 'breasts, vaginas, clitorises,' hormones and so on, or the physical processes of menstruation, pregnancy, childbirth or lactation that constitute female bodies. Rather, these are constituted by the rules that structure these physical processes, and by the objects, physical spaces, institutions and practices that result from past human action taking place against this background of social objects and structures. This makes the female body a rule-bound body, defined by particular meanings and possibilities (p. 28).

Clothes are also objects in the series gender, as are cosmetics, tools and the physical separation between male and female spaces. Young writes: 'I may discover myself "as a woman" by being on the "wrong" dorm floor' (p. 29).

In addition to social objects, the series gender is constituted by structures that organize these objects. Young discusses two of these, enforced heterosexuality and the sexual division of labor, which themselves create a multitude of objects and spaces that further reproduce the series (pp. 28, 29).

When they act, men and women take this background into account, even if not in a conscious manner. Self-conscious groups can arise from the social reality of gender. Not all these groups, however, are feminist groups. Young gives an example, from Meredith Tax's novel *Rivington Street*, of a group of Russian-Jewish immigrant women, who organize a boycott of the local merchant who has manipulated the chicken market to increase his profits. This group arises from the women's serialized existence defined by the sexual division of labor. It also arises from their serialized existence as shoppers and as Russian-Jewish working-class immigrants. But it is not a feminist group (p. 34).

Feminist groups, Young proposes, are groups who at least implicitly refer to the series of women. They draw on the experience of living within the series of gender, which is multilayered and has a wide variety of aspects. Different feminist groups take up different aspects or parts of the series of gender, which explains the diversity of feminism. At the same time, what makes them all feminist groups is that they refer to the series itself. Groups of women – feminist and not – will always be partial in relation to the series – because when women come together as groups, their womanliness is not the only thing that brings them together (p. 36).

Race as seriality

Like gender, race, I would like to suggest, is a series. In saying this I claim that there is a unity to race. But this unity is not constituted by a shared black culture, a shared set of interests, or shared features intrinsic to individuals. Rather, the unity of race is constituted by a social practice. However, the series race cannot be reduced to Gooding-Williams's social practice of classification of persons into black or white. For in addition to this practice of classification, the series race encompasses material objects, the rules that structure them and the institutions, spaces and practices developed through the actions oriented toward these objects and structured by these rules. The series race performs a distinction between black (or raced) and white persons, a distinction not determined by intrinsic qualities of persons, but by the shared constellation of objects, rules and practices that give different orientations to black and white bodies. But while the series performs this distinction, the series is nevertheless shared by all social actors that inhabit it, regardless of the racial position they are assigned in the series. The series is shared in the sense that it structures the action of both black and white persons; it is part of the background of action for both black and white persons.

What are the objects and the structures of the series race?

Black bodies – male and female – are among the objects of the series race. Like female bodies, black bodies are not constituted simply by physical facts. Rather, they are constituted by rules, rules created over time, and that have changed over time. These rules and the ongoing action instituting them have created practices and spaces, institutions and environments where these rules are constantly reiterated, such as the barber-shops for men and beauty parlors for women, the practice of strengthening hair, the practice of the Afro hair, the association between black bodies and athleticism, black neighborhoods, urban segregation, black churches, etc.

As female bodies are created within the structures of enforced heterosexuality, black bodies, male and female, are created through rules governing the reproduction of black bodies and the sexual, familial and intimate relationships between black persons and persons of other races. They have varied over time, and have depended on the particular system of domination in place at that time. They have created practices like the breaking of slave families, white masters' access to the bodies of black female slaves, forced sterilization of black American women, criminalization of mixed-race marriages, legally mandated contraception, etc. (Roberts, 1999).

I want to suggest that there are at least two other structures that organize the social (practico-inert) objects of the series race, structures that interact to each other. I will call them 'the racial structure of labor' and 'the racial structure of law.'

The racial structure of labor has to be understood in the historical context defined by slavery and its effects, over time, on the physical environment. It includes, for example, structures that relegate menial, low-skilled and domestic labor to black persons, as well as the structure of differential educational opportunities, reflected in, among others, segregated school systems, affirmative action policies, and historically black colleges.

This understanding of race enables inquiry into the connections between race and the structures that organize labor and the production of wealth in a capitalist economy with, for example, its low rewards for low-skilled work. And further, it enables an analysis of the connections between race and patterns of residential segregation, norms of work-residential segregation, transportation policy, etc.

Similarly, the racial structure of law has to be understood as the effects, over time, of slavery and Jim Crow segregation. Currently, mass incarceration of a disproportionately large black population and the growth of the prison system are parts of this structure.

Understood in this way, as a series, the unity of race is constituted by the *practico-inert* reality of a complex, multilayered and interlocking constellation of objects and social practices and rules that structure them and that our action is oriented toward. This is unity at the impersonal level. Understood in this way, the unity of race brings together not only all black Americans, but all Americans, because they all share the 'practico-inert' reality of the series race, as a common background for their actions. The series race can be the basis of solidarity for action across the racial division between black and white Americans.

This way of understanding unity is also compatible with the diversity of black political life. The diversity comes from the self-conscious groups that can be created on the basis of the series. They will always be partial in relation to the series. Not all of these will be anti-racist. Like feminist groups, anti-racist groups are those who reference the reality of race as a series that, in some way, even implicitly, thematize it and attempt to change it. Different anti-racist groups will take on different parts of the complex reality of the series, and as a result will pursue different goals and aims, and will use different means.

However, all black groups will be united by the fact that they arise from the social reality of the series race. All anti-racist groups will be further united by the fact that they reference the series of race. This unity of the series from which groups arise can be a basis for solidarity. I call this form of solidarity 'racial structural solidarity.' For individuals, it is solidarity in an impersonal sense: in virtue of inhabiting the same structure, of having the same social structure to orient thier actions. For different black groups, it is solidarity in virtue of the fact that they arise out of the same social reality. And for anti-racist groups, it is in addition solidarity in virtue of refering to the same social reality, even when they focus on different parts of the complex reality of the series race. This is solidarity across different political purposes, methods, strategies, and priorities. But it is not forged through political action. Rather, it is an expression of the social reality that gives rise to political action, including political action that aims to transform that social reality.

Conclusion

I have argued that questions of solidarity for collective action against racial oppression have to be preceded by social-theoretical questions about the social reality that our collective action aims to change. 'Race as seriality,' a concept I developed in analogy with Iris Young's 'gender as seriality,' provides such a descriptive approach, I argued, one that can ground a notion of solidarity on one's shared structural, impersonal situation. This provides an alternative to notions of solidarity based on one's identity, on one's experience with racial prejudice as well as to notions of solidarity forged in action.

Notes

1. http://www.theatlantic.com/politics/archive/2016/01/bernie-sanders-reparations/424602/checked on May 5, 2016.
2. Seehttps://www.jacobinmag.com/2016/03/reparations-ta-nehisi-coates-cedric-johnson-bernie-sanders/, https://www.jacobinmag.com/2016/03/cedric-johnson-brian-jones-ta-nehisi-coates-reparations/, http://www.theatlantic.com/politics/archive/2016/01/bernie-sanders-right-on-reparations/426,720/, http://www.theatlantic.com/politics/archive/2016/02/why-we-write/459,909/, checked on May 5, 2016.
3. https://www.jacobinmag.com/2016/02/ta-nehisi-coates-case-for-reparations-bernie-sanders-racism/, p. 14.
4. Shelby (2005, p. 156) does, however, argue that the non-consensus issues should be supported because they can affect racism against everyone. See Gooding-Williams (2009, pp. 228–230) for a criticism of this argument.

Acknowledgments

I want to thank Andrew Dilts, Avigail Ferdman, Michaele Ferguson, Bob Gooding-Williams, Waheed Hussain, Peggy Kohn, Avery Kolers and Daniel Silver, as well as the two anonymous reviewers for this journal for suggestions and discussions of the ideas in this paper.

Disclosure statement

No potential conflict of interest was reported by the author.

References

Balfour, L. (2006). Review of Tommie Shelby, We who are dark: The philosophical foundations of black solidarity. *Symposia on gender, race and philosophy*. Cambridge, MA: Harvard University Press, 2005. Book reviews. Retrieved from http://web.mit.edu/sgrp

Gooding-Williams, R. (1998). Race, multiculturalism and democracy. *Constellations, 5*(1), 18–41.

Gooding-Williams, R. (2009). *In the shadow of Du Bois Afro-American political thought in America*. Cambridge, MA: Harvard University Press.

Hacking, I. (1986). Making up people. In T. C. Heller, M. Sosna, & D. Wellbery (Eds.), *Reconstructing individualism* (pp. 222–236). Stanford: Stanford University Press.

Roberts, D. (1999). *Killing the black body. Race, reproduction and the meaning of liberty*. New York, NY: Vintage Books.

Sartre, J.-P. (1995). *Anti-semite and Jew*. (G. Becker, Trans.). With an introduction by Michael Walzer. New York, NY: Schocken Books.

Shelby, T. (2002, January). Foundations of black solidarity: Collective identity or common oppression? *Ethics, 112*, 231–266.

Shelby, T. (2005). *We who are dark. The philosophical foundations of black solidarity*. Cambridge, MA: Harvard University Press.

Young, I. (1997). Gender as seriality: Thinking about women as a social collective. In *Intersecting voices. Dilemmas of gender, political philosophy, and policy* (pp. 22–23). Princeton, NJ: Princeton University Press.

What undermines solidarity? Four approaches and their implications for contemporary political theory

Charles H. T. Lesch

ABSTRACT

Solidarity is crucial for realizing justice, securing public goods, and reducing domination. Yet there have been few theoretical studies of its threats and vulnerabilities. In this paper I fill this lacuna, outlining four approaches to what undermines solidarity and considering their implications for contemporary political theory. I begin by reviewing the empirical literature on solidarity, noting that its focus on diversity and individuation has yielded inconclusive results. I then develop four alternative threats to solidarity by drawing from the history of political thought, social theory, and religious studies: interpersonal dependence (Jean-Jacques Rousseau); radical evil (Immanuel Kant); self-dissolution (Émile Durkheim); and moral spectatorship (Emmanuel Levinas). Taking these threats into account, I conclude, should significantly impact our normative theorizing about solidarity. In particular, it should encourage a research agenda that attends to solidarity's affective, esthetic, and non-rational sources.

Solidarity: uses and threats

Solidarity is crucial for realizing justice, securing public goods, and reducing domination. As Margaret Kohn (this issue, pp. 4, 15–16) has argued, societies with a high degree of solidarity are more likely to guarantee their citizens the necessities of a decent life and have reduced levels of interpersonal dependence and exploitation. Others in this special issue have spotlighted solidarity's utility for combating racial injustice (Marin, this issue), pushing for environmental protections (Kolers, this issue), and motivating majority groups to support the public goods of social minorities (Ferdman, this issue).

These studies speak to solidarity's *uses*. They add to an important body of literature on its critical but underappreciated role for creating decent societies.

Yet despite the renewed attention paid to solidarity and a growing awareness of its centrality for political theory, there have been surprisingly few normative analyses of its threats and vulnerabilities.

My aim in this paper is to help fill this lacuna. Taking solidarity's significance as a given, I ask a different question: What *undermines* solidarity? What weakens or jeopardizes social unity? Or put another way, what should theorists eager to channel solidarity's potential toward positive moral outcomes be worried about in crafting their normative models?

This question can be refined further. For the concept of solidarity itself, in addition to having been defined in a number of different ways historically, can also be evaluated from at least two distinct perspectives. From one vantage, solidarity is an *objective description* of the particular form that a society assumes on a macro-scale (Tönnies, 1887/1957; Weber, 1921/1978). To speak of solidarity in this sense is to adopt a bird's eye view of a group of people and attempt to take a snapshot, using different metrics, of the strength of its members' attachments to one another. Work of this kind has often focused on two factors in particular: the impact of cultural and ethnic diversity, and the effects of 'individualization.' In both cases, the findings have been indeterminate. For example, Merlin Schaeffer (2014) and Tom Van der Meer and Jochem Tolsma (2014) have demonstrated through meta-analyses that just as many studies have pointed to a non-impact of diversity on solidarity as studies that have implied a detrimental impact. Genov Nikolai (2013), while raising urgent questions about the potentially deleterious effects of individualization on solidarity, likewise notes that nothing firm has been established.

Given the inconclusive state of the empirical literature, this paper offers four new diagnoses of the threats to solidarity by drawing from the history of political thought, social theory, and religious studies. Each of these diagnoses uses a second method for evaluating solidarity: as a description of *subjective sentiments* related to commitment and motivation that people have toward one another. Rather than describing large social formations, they focus on the micro-level of individual psychology. Though these diagnoses themselves cannot be conclusively proven, they are potentially valuable in at least two ways. First, they fulfill one of the important functions of political theory: to conceptualize new avenues for research that can later be taken up by social scientists (Thompson, 2008). While they focus on the individual, they are potentially scalable by scholars looking to break the empirical stalemate. Second, precisely because they direct themselves to the inner workings of the self rather than to society as a whole, they help to reveal the causal mechanisms responsible for undermining solidarity. Consequently, for both political theorists and scholars in public policy, they suggest paths forward not only for recognizing the causes of social pathology, but also for finding its remedy.

In each section of this paper, I focus on one of these four diagnoses, probing its underlying moral psychology and larger-scale social consequences. I arrive at each one via an interpretation and rational reconstruction of a thinker: *interpersonal dependence* (Jean-Jacques Rousseau); *radical evil* (Immanuel Kant); *self-dissolution* (Émile Durkheim); and *moral spectatorship* (Emmanuel Levinas). I focus on these particular thinkers for two main reasons: First, I believe that each offers an under-expressed perspective on the forces undermining solidarity. Other historically important analysts of solidarity, like Thomas Hobbes, already have a prominent voice in contemporary political science. Second, each of these thinkers is to an uncommon extent in direct dialog with the others. Each learns from his predecessor, builds off of his thought, and attempts to resolve his perceived flaws and weaknesses. In proceeding, therefore, I note that in certain cases these diagnoses are at odds with one another, while in others they can be adopted together.

In concluding the paper, I propose one or more lessons that scholars of solidarity might take from each one. I also derive a more general recommendation for contemporary political theory: If we are to respond to solidarity's threats, and even enhance our salutary social bonds, we need to attend more closely to the role of the non-rational parts of human psychology in structuring how human beings make and are inspired to act on their commitments to one another.

Rousseau and interpersonal dependence

According to Rousseau, the primary force undermining solidarity is interpersonal dependence and its attendant pathologies: competition, exploitation, and domination. He arrives at this view through a psychological-historical account of humanity's social development. Human beings, he argues, are naturally 'good' in the sense that they have no intrinsically antisocial tendencies (1754/2010, p. 197). If a person's needs are met, she will be happy and have no reason to seek conflict with others (1762/1979, pp. 81–82). Thus, in contrast to theorists like Machiavelli and Nietzsche, who regard a certain subset of individuals as born social predators, Rousseau believes that all human beings are naturally peaceful. And in contrast to Hobbes, who sees the drive for vainglory and domination as a basic facet of human psychology, he understands the craving for power, too, as historically contingent and 'unnatural.' Dependence arises because in actually existing human societies the balance between the needs human beings have and their ability to satisfy them is continually disrupted.

He provides two reasons for this disruption, one economic and pragmatic, the other social and psychological. First, with the advent of the division of labor, each person becomes a specialist in her respective area of work. She loses her capacity to procure her own needs and so becomes materially dependent on others (1754/2010, pp. 151, 159, 165, 167). Second and more important, in society new needs are generated over and above the physical, foremost among them positive social evaluation or 'esteem.' Exposed to the evaluative gaze of others, a human being comes to intuit how her actions appear in their eyes, exchanging her first-person perspective for a third-person one (1754/2010, pp. 187–188). She learns what the sociologist Erving Goffman (1959, p. 3), in his classic study of everyday self-presentation, called the 'arts of impression management': the ability to sway others by attuning one's public appearance to their needs and expectations. But although mastering these arts seems advantageous, Rousseau emphasizes that they come with a curse. Once we develop a taste for being evaluated, our sense of worth becomes irrevocably tied to this evaluation. And because our evaluation and status can come only from other people, we become dependent on their company to satisfy our desire for esteem.

Our dependence on esteem produces three social and political pathologies harmful to our solidarity.

First, on an interpersonal level, it ensures that the realization of our own interests can only come at the expense of our fellows. The problem is that esteem is a scarce resource. Because social status is relative, the aggrandizement of a subset of the populace necessarily entails the diminishment of another subset. This would not present a dilemma as long as people acceded to their comparatively lower stature, living, in Marx's famous term, in conditions of 'false consciousness.' But in the society Rousseau uses as his template, one witnessing the end of feudal structures and a new egalitarian ethos – and certainly in our own – it poses a major challenge. Esteem in such circumstances has become much more of a universal need. Fulfilling our own needs requires denying others the ability to fulfill their own. And this makes us antisocial, pitting us against our neighbors and actively undermining their projects and ambitions (1754/2010, pp. 170–171, 198–200).

Second, on a political level, our dependence on positive social judgment exacerbates the disjuncture between our own perceived interests and the interests of the polity as a whole. Instead of directing our thoughts toward the common good, and directing our energies toward its realization, we think about and work for ourselves above all. By encouraging selfishness, the hunger for esteem thus undermines unity, stymies collective projects, and denudes everyday relations of affection and self-sacrifice (1752/2010, pp. 99–100).

Our dependence on esteem also gives rise to a third force deeply harmful of solidarity: interpersonal domination. In society, we cannot satisfy our needs by our own power. Nonetheless, a solution presents itself: Perhaps, we can do so with the help of other people. And to ensure that these others serve us rather than themselves, we endeavor to keep them as much as possible under our control. This is the thinking underlying the desire to dominate: If we enlist a sufficient number of others, and control them thoroughly enough, we will finally have what it takes to be able to free ourselves of dependence. Though we are individually weak, this thinking goes, we can be socially strong.

These dynamics of interpersonal dependence produce a dire cumulative effect: the deterioration of affection, attachment, and solidarity. Having experienced the 'pleasure of dominating' – its utility for fulfilling our needs – we want to do it more. We become, as Rousseau declares with a rhetorical flourish, like 'ravenous wolves which once they have tasted human flesh scorn all other food, and from then on want to devour only men' (1754/2010, p. 171, cf. 1762/1979, pp. 68, 228). One of the reasons that people are willing to put up with being oppressed and dominated, Rousseau notes, is because of the hope that they themselves will one day have the opportunity to oppress and dominate (1754/2010, p. 183, cf. 1762/1979, p. 87). It matters little that the promise of freedom held by domination is in fact a fantasy. As Hegel will later point out in his famous chapter on 'Herrschaft und Knechtschaft,' commonly referred to as the 'master-slave dialectic,' there is an irony to domination: Those who seek to dominate do so because it promises to free them from dependence on others; but because their status and power depend on the judgment of those they dominate, in practice they become more dependent. Thus while it is surely true, as Hussain (this issue) has argued in this issue, that solidarity can help attenuate the socially detrimental effects of capitalistic competition, it is equally true, as Rousseau shows, that such competition can quickly deplete our existing stores of social commitment.

Kant and radical evil

'Radical evil' is Kant's explanation for what undermines solidarity. It is also his direct alternative and response to Rousseau's account. According to Kant, Rousseau's view of social pathology contains a fatal flaw: It fails to make space for genuine moral freedom. It implies that human beings are like natural phenomena, fated to either dominate or not dominate others based on an arbitrary, externally determined balance between their needs and ability to fulfill them (Kant, 1793/2004, 6:21). Such a view renders 'evil' as nothing more than the mechanistic by-product of social alchemy. And it renders our larger solidarity, too, as ultimately deterministic and beyond human control. For Kant, therefore, it must be the case that social pathology is not determined by dependence but chosen. It is not the result of the 'sensuous nature of the human being' but a 'deed of freedom' (1793/2004, 6:21). It stems from what Kant calls our 'free power of choice': our ability to decide, with a transcendental 'absolute spontaneity,' to act according to a moral maxim instead of a non-moral one (1793/2004, 6:34–35). Moral maxims are determined by reason. And so another way to describe Kant's moral theory is that a person acts freely ('autonomously') when she uses her absolutely spontaneous power of choice to decide in favor of reason rather than non-reason.

But here Kant must deal with a problem: If we choose between right and wrong with absolute spontaneity, why do we so often choose wrong? If our ability to act morally is wholly undetermined by our self-serving interests, desires, and inclinations, why do we usually let them prevail over reason? Why, in short, is immorality so common and morality so rare? Or to pose the problem on a macro-scale: Given that every human being *can* always choose to act with respect, love, and solidarity toward her fellows, why are human societies *in fact* so often plagued by antagonism, exploitation, and domination?

Kant's answer is the 'radical evil' of humanity. Our tendency for antisocial behavior, he argues, stems not from our sociality but our absolute spontaneity. Contra Rousseau, it is a result not of our transition from an isolated 'natural' condition to a social 'civilized' one, but of a flaw in our deep-seated capacity to make moral decisions undetermined by the laws of nature. It is contained within our very 'free power of choice' itself. In Kant's technical language, it is the 'propensity of the power of choice to maxims that subordinate the incentives of the moral law to others (not moral ones)' (1793/2004, 6:30). What makes humanity's evil 'radical' for Kant, therefore, is not, as it will later be for Arendt, that it is especially depraved (1951/1994, p. 443). It is that human beings, at the most fundamental level of their moral psychology, have a 'propensity' to choose to act in a non-moral rather than moral way.

While radical evil is Kant's way of diagnosing the moral psychological *causes* of what undermines solidarity, he uses a different term to describe its real-world social *effects*: unsocial sociability. In other words, for Kant unsocial sociability is the empirical result of humanity's transcendental radical evil. He coins the term in his *Idea for a Universal History with a Cosmopolitan Purpose*, defining it as the 'tendency [of human beings] to come together in society, coupled... with a continual resistance which constantly threatens to break this society up' (1784/2008, p. 44). Though he does not use the words 'radical evil' in this essay, he does note that unsocial sociability is 'rooted in human nature' (1784/2008, p. 44). And he explicitly frames the work as connecting moral philosophy to social theory. The aim of *Universal History*, he writes, is to examine the 'will's manifestations in the world of phenomena,' to consider the 'free exercise of the human will on a large scale' (1784/2008, p. 41). That is, its purpose, and the purpose of the concept of unsocial sociability, is to assess the social ramifications of our radically evil power of free choice.

Here another important difference emerges between Rousseau and Kant. For Rousseau, nothing inevitably undermines solidarity. Social pathology comes into being neither because it reflects inescapable feature of our sociability, nor because it is ingrained in human nature, but rather because of contingent features of civilization. Thus when individuals are properly educated or societies are properly organized, antisocial behaviors like domination can be minimized or eliminated. For Kant, by contrast, our radical evil *necessarily* leads us to try to make others dependent on our will. Once in society, a person is invariably driven to acquire 'honor, power, or property.' He cannot but seek 'status among his fellows' in order to secure for himself a position of higher standing relative to others (1784/2008, p. 44).

In *Universal History*, therefore, Kant describes a social dynamic similarly destructive to solidarity as that cataloged by Rousseau, but updated for his novel moral psychology. While an individual 'cannot bear' other people, dependent as he is on their evaluation, he also 'cannot bear to leave' them (1784/2008, p. 44). Because of his radical evil, his craving for social standing is both miserable and insatiable. And to achieve such standing, he debases himself. He is willing to adopt all of the most lowly traits of character, including 'ambition,' 'tyranny,' and 'greed.' Not surprisingly, such vices, when scaled up, create societies marked by jealousy, competition, and 'continual antagonism' (1784/2008, p. 45). 'The human being,' Kant writes a few years later, destroys the possibility of his own happiness 'by means of plagues that he invents for himself.' The 'oppression of domination' and the 'barbarism of war' come not from a distortion of any putatively 'natural' condition. They come from the 'nature inside us' (1790/2000, 5:430). They are the inescapable products of our radical evil.

Durkheim and self-dissolution

Durkheim develops his diagnosis of what undermines solidarity via a critique of Kant's social theory. Where Kant argues that the basic categories of normativity are shared by all human beings, Durkheim, in *The Elementary forms of Religious Life*, stresses their origins in social – and especially religious – experience (1912/1995, pp. 9, 15, 238). The philosopher's failure to grasp this fact, Durkheim argues, is in fact responsible for a fundamental aporia in his mature moral psychology: his inability to answer the question 'Why be moral?' Kant, as we have seen, answers this conundrum through his concept of absolute spontaneity: Without knowing how or why, we decide whether to adopt moral maxims with a transcendental freedom. According to Durkheim, however, this appeal to the transcendental signals a major failure on the part of Kant to grasp the essence of human social bonds. To the ethically indifferent, the mere existence of freedom has no appeal. Rational morality will seem as little more than a series of formal rules, barren of meaning and authority. It will lack *force*, the power to inspire a person to act, to bind her to duty, to spur her to transcend her egoism and sacrifice for others (1912/1995, pp. 202, 205–206). For Durkheim, therefore, Kant's philosophy implies something untenable: That the *meaning* of what is moral can be divorced from the *motivation* to be moral.

Durkheim's response is to stress the role played by one form of social religious experience in the particular: our desire for the 'sacred.' Human beings, he argues against both Rousseau and Kant, desire not only material welfare and interpersonal recognition. They also long for things like the metaphysical and the transcendent. They crave esthetic objects that surpass their individual existence and mundane reality. The sacred's function, for Durkheim, is thus to provide a locus for this metaphysical desire (1912/1995, p. 229).

In doing so, the sacred also fulfills a second and more critical task for Durkheim: securing the community's solidarity. Feelings of normative commitment and motivation do not arise in a vacuum. A person only becomes capable of true self-transcendence when such feelings are channeled into material things, when they go through a process of 'settling upon external objects' (1912/1995, p. 421). One straightforward example of this process of sacralization is a symbol, like a totem or ritual article (1912/1995, pp. 220–232). Thus when we speak of someone pledging allegiance – or dying – 'for the flag,' it is not the flag itself to which we are referring but rather its symbolic content as a sacred object. The flag both embodies that individual's solidarity with her community and provides a way to channel her desire for transcendence toward its collective ends.

Yet for all its socially salutary effects, participation in the sacred also carries a profound danger for solidarity: self-dissolution. One of the sacred's attractions is its ability to powerfully channel humanity's desire for transcendence toward positive ends. It can inspire in human beings a willingness to move beyond their self-interest and sacrifice for others. But such forms of self-transcendence are also morally hazardous. For when a person finds herself in the grip of the sacred, the line dividing her sense of self and her reality may collapse. As described most famously by the philosopher of religion Rudolf Otto (1917/1958, pp. 22, 193), certain modes of religious or quasi-religious experience can lead to a craving for 'submergence and absorption in the "wholly other,"' a longing to fully dissolve the boundary separating oneself from her surroundings. And this kind of self-dissolution holds two related threats to social cohesion.

First, self-dissolution can cause people to momentarily lose their basic sense of normative constraint. Even outside of straightforwardly 'religious' contexts, it can inspire them to take actions toward others that are disrespectful, exploitative, or violent. As Jonathan Glover (2012, pp. 47–118) notes in his history of twentieth-century violence, for example, military units tasked with killing civilians would sometimes engage in rituals designed to submerge their members' sense of self and relieve their moral qualms. And in *Dialectic of Enlightenment*, Theodor Adorno and Max Horkheimer describe how Hitler drew the massed Nazi crowds into a frenzy through his carefully choreographed imagery and public performance of primitivist rage (1947/2002, pp. 150–153).

Self-dissolution's second threat to solidarity has to do with the mythic mind-set that it engenders. The sacred is an esthetic quality. While it can be marshaled for positive or negative social ends, it has no intrinsic normative content. And what this means is that its authority, having been accepted in a ritual context, can no longer be challenged for its *truth* or *justification*. It cannot be questioned. It commands simply because it commands. Consequently, the very qualities of the sacred that inspire solidaristic self-sacrifice – its holy distance and detachment from the mundane – also dissolve the self's capacity for independent judgment. They risk serving radically inegalitarian and anti-democratic ends that compromise solidarity. The sociologist Peter Berger (1969, pp. 3–29) has described how this happens through his analysis of 'objectifica-tion.' Sacred objects, including norms and beliefs, are our own creations. Yet over time, we forget this fact. And as we do, these norms and beliefs come to appear as 'objective,' that is, unalterable, governed by fate, and a kind of 'second nature.' As Karl Polanyi (1944/2001, p. 75) has famously described, for example, highly historically contingent features of capitalism that tore apart European communities came to be conceived as immutable, the market's equivalent of natural laws. Thus in addition to momentarily removing our normative con-straints, self-dissolution also has the potential to perform ideological functions that undermine our commitment and attachment to one another.

Levinas and moral spectatorship

Though Levinas shares Durkheim's moral psychology and concern for self-dis-solution, the threat to solidarity that he identifies is almost a direct inversion of his predecessor's. On an everyday basis, he notes, the problem with liberal democracy is not too much self-transcendence. Human beings in late capitalism do not generally experience an over-intensity of solidaristic feeling. We have the opposite challenge: a profound moral indifference. It is not merely that we lack the *motivation* to respond to others' privations. On a deeper level, we actually *fail to see* our neighbors as subjects of individual moral responsibility. The culprit, according to Levinas, is a cognitive shift. As participants in large-scale systems of law and economic redistribution, we always run the risk of adopting for ourselves the perspective of these systems themselves. When we do so, we assume an abstract, bird's eye perspective on human solidarity. We outsource our ethical responsibility to these systems, becoming incapable of experiencing actually - existing people as having claims on our moral attention. We turn into moral spectators, losing our sense of personal accountability to our neighbors. And in the aggregate, Levinas suggests, the societies that arise out of such moral spectatorship are characterized by brittle social bonds. They harbor individuals who are consumed with their own interests and unwilling to sacrifice for others' needs.

Levinas traces the causes of moral spectatorship to a basic aspect of cog-nition: our faculty for conceptualization, that is, our use of abstract ideas and categories. Concepts for Levinas are a double-edged sword. On the one hand, they permit us to navigate our world in a complex and orderly way. Instead of encountering reality one particular object at a time – one tall leafy thing fol-lowed by another tall leafy thing – a concept allows us to group these objects together: trees. In this sense, the faculty of conceptualization is indispensa-ble for an important aspect of our solidarity: social democratic institutions (Crepaz, 2008). These institutions, after all, necessarily function by means of bureaucracies that are dependent upon a conceptual epistemology. Levinas, generally a supporter of redistributive policies, recognizes the necessity of this kind of thinking. He does not take issue with conceptualization in and of itself.

On the other hand, Levinas argues that using concepts outside of their proper context can be morally dangerous: By allowing us to adopt as *individuals* the frame of mind of these social and political *institutions*, concepts risk diverting our attention away from flesh-and-blood persons. To conceptualize a thing is by definition to efface its particularity. It is to weaken its status as a unique object of perception and transform it into the mere instance of a category (1961/1969, p. 46). Such a practice is certainly indispensable for a functioning bureaucracy. But transposed into the ethical epistemology of an individual, it leads to a diminution of responsibility. No longer will a person see herself as a particular and embodied self, with obligations and responsibilities to persons in her immediate surroundings. Instead of adopting the second-person perspective of everyday ethical life, she will adopt the third-person perspective of the social system as a whole. In other words, she will abstract herself outward from her present circumstances, interpreting her actions not in themselves, but as parts of larger social and historical structures (1974/2002, p. 92). At the cognitive level, she may be abstractly joined to many others – even to a universal humanity. Yet, such an impersonal moral psychology will not only fail to equip her for situations that require her moral attention; it will produce ethical indifference, blinding her to the suffering taking place before her very eyes (1974/2002, pp. 196–197 note). She will become a moral spectator.

Take an everyday example, like encountering an impoverished person on the street. Levinas is concerned that when confronted by such a person, I will not really see the unique, suffering human being in front of me. Instead, armed with my faculty of conceptualization, I will perceive merely an instantiation of the more general category of 'indigent,' a category that is itself part of a larger social framework. Thinking this way, I might assume the perspective of the economic system as a whole. And from this vantage, impoverished people become simply an inevitable outgrowth of a system that, taken in sum, supposedly maximizes pleasure and minimizes pain. Indeed from a sufficiently global perspective on human affairs, my giving to this person might be seen as *tampering* with this system, distorting economic incentives that produce the best outcomes overall.

When we start to think in this way, Levinas suggests, we have lost something important. To use his term of art, we no longer see the 'face' of the other. We think impartially, in concepts and categories, like the system itself. And the upshot for our solidarity is a moral spectatorship, a society in which 'no being looks at the face of the other, but all beings negate one another' (1961/1969, p. 222).

Implications for contemporary political theory

In this paper, I offered four new approaches to what undermines solidarity by culling from the history of political thought, social theory, and religious studies. For Rousseau, social pathology arises as human beings find themselves dependent on their growing needs, esteem foremost among them. Kant shares Rousseau's picture of society's ills, but locates their cause elsewhere: humanity's 'radical evil,' its innate moral psychological propensity to prioritize non-moral (and frequently selfish) maxims over moral ones. Durkheim, highlighting a weakness in Kant's moral theory, identifies an additional threat to solidarity: self-dissolution. Human beings, he argues, have an innate desire for transcendence and receptivity to the 'sacred.' Yet while such forms of experience (both religious and secular) can be socially beneficial, they also risk violently dissolving our moral constraints and reproducing a mythic mind-set. Levinas does not deny the dangers of self-dissolution. But he suggests that in modern liberal capitalism, solidarity is more frequently undermined by a more quotidian moral spectatorship. Abstract juridical and economic systems are today responsible for so many social functions that we have a tendency to entirely outsource our ethical responsibility, failing to attend to the needs and vulnerabilities of the concrete, flesh-and-blood people that we encounter in daily life.

These approaches, I believe, hold a number of lessons for theorists of solidarity. To uncover them, however, it is first necessary to briefly survey the leading normative models of solidarity in contemporary political theory. We might refer to these models broadly speaking as *ideology based* and *identity based*.

Ideology-based models argue that the kind of normative commitment and psychological motivation necessary for securing solidarity should be realizable through allegiance to shared political principles alone. According to John Rawls' (1993/2005) idea of a liberal value consensus, for example, solidarity emerges automatically when members of a polity reflect rationally on the principles of liberal democratic justice. Thus, even in diverse societies, citizens will be committed to one another because of their shared beliefs, arrived at through reason, about the principles underlying liberal democracy. A second ideology-based model is the theory of 'constitutional patriotism' advanced by Jürgen Habermas (1992/1998, 2009, 2012, cf. Müller, 2007; Stilz, 2009). According to this view, laws are just when they emerge from our reasoned deliberation in common, and, as products of our own will and values, they will necessarily command our allegiance and motivation.

Identity-based models reject this view, arguing that there is a gap in any purely ideological form of solidarity that must be filled by a pre-political sense of identity and commitment. A first kind of identity-based model is liberal nationalism. As championed by Yael Tamir (1993), David Miller (1995), and others (Gans, 2003; Nussbaum, 2013), liberal nationalism emphasizes the necessity of 'thicker' forms of commonalty like culture, ethnicity, and memory. This sense of belonging, in turn, is infused into the institutions, laws, and symbols of the polity. A second identity-based model is the liberal multiculturalism associated most prominently with Will Kymlicka (2001). Kymlicka argues that while a polity's identity should be forged around a unified story, claims of national allegiance should be sufficiently 'thinned' so as to simultaneously provide for the public recognition and legal protection of minority groups.

Although Rousseau and Kant disagree about the underlying causes of social pathology, both might cast doubt on the claim by ideology-based theorists that solidarity will emerge organically out of any liberal democratic political system, no matter how rational or deliberative. Every society has informal power relations in which some are dominant and others quiescent. If left unchecked, these forms of dependence will create a dynamic that is ripe for exploitation, abuse, and domination. They will lead not only to macro-scale social instabilities, but to micro-scale cruelties of the kind that Judith Shklar (1984, 37) famously believed that we need to put 'first' on our list of 'ordinary vices.' Such products of dependence are inimical to the forms of everyday social trust and respect that are needed for solidarity. And they are not eliminable by shared political principles or deliberative practices alone.

The threat posed by Durkheimian self-dissolution, by contrast, applies primarily to identity-based models. Although such models can be benign for periods of time, they always risk the problems associated with the sacred. To begin with, by elevating one nation, ethnicity, or religion above others, they either directly or indirectly stifle critical thinking. They diminish our moral responsibility, replacing our own critical judgment with predetermined norms. And they demand – or strongly imply – that certain matters, like the state's organizing identity, are akin to a sacred object, holding a mythical status out of bounds for critique. At the same time, by valorizing a form of community that has no inherent moral status, identify-based models risk stirring members to undertake acts of self-transcendence that serve causes that are morally dubious or plainly evil. They militarize forms of collective identity, using rituals, songs, symbols, and other markers of 'imagined community' to submerge the self into a larger 'we' (Anderson, 1983/2006). It is not without reason that nationalism, in Bernard Yack's (2012, p. 303) pithy phrase, 'has a high body count.'

Levinasian moral spectatorship applies equally to ideology-based and identity-based models. For the former, it alerts us to the problems associated with grounding social bonds too heavily on shared allegiance to abstract principles. Such bonds are not only fragile and ineffective, suffering from what Aristotle (1996, p. 1262b), in his critique of Plato's ideal city, called 'diluted' motivation. As Levinas shows, in certain cases they *actively contribute* to the diminution of our solidarity, encouraging us to outsource our responsibility to large-scale economic and juridical systems. By rewiring our moral cognition in overly conceptual terms, they detach us from the urgent needs of actually existing people. Moral spectatorship is also a risk for identity-based models. In the same way that a member of a liberal capitalist society may delegate her ethical judgment to state institutions and market forces, the nationalist risks delegating her judgment to whatever is deemed to be in her nation's interest. She potentially renounces any accountability she may have to individually assess her moral choices.

Each of these four approaches suggests different causal mechanisms for what undermines solidarity and so offer diverse insights for political theorists seeking remedies to social pathology. To be sure, their psychological portraits should not be taken uncritically. They are each vulnerable to objections, as their critiques of one another show. Yet even if we might take issue with aspects of their analyses, I believe that they together point to a more general oversight in contemporary political theory: Solidarity, even in liberal democratic societies, may not be fully derivable through reason alone. It is true that identity-based theorists recognize this to a degree, arguing that polities need the 'nation' to provide an affective basis for our social bond. But however much it is hemmed-in by philosophical constraints, even 'safe nationalism' (Nussbaum, 2013, p. 69) can always turn to chauvinism. Ideology-based models, by contrast, risk not only a shriveled social bond, but a much more profound problem. For if there are aspects of our commitment and motivation that are stubbornly irreducible to reason, ignoring or suppressing them may lead to their being exploited by illiberal and antidemocratic forms of solidarity.

The most promising path forward, therefore, may lie in Durkheim's insight into humanity's innate desire for self-transcendence. No doubt, this desire contains real risks, as Durkheim himself points out. And so it is understandable that some theorists, Habermas most prominent among them, have rejected this path and sought to reground social unity along rational-deliberative lines. But if the non-rational elements of the psyche are properly channeled – not into nationalist political allegiance, but into our everyday ethical relations with others – they may also hold the key to a new model for solidarity. Such an ethical solidarity would deliver the power of self-transcendence without the moral dangers of nationalism; it would press us to actively combat interpersonal dependence and exploitation; and it would inspire us to overcome our moral indifference and take individual responsibility for the vulnerabilities of our fellow human beings. If political theorists wish to leverage our social bonds toward realizing justice, diminishing dependence, and securing public goods, it is such a model of ethical solidarity that they must seek out.

Acknowledgements

I owe a deep debt of gratitude to Peggy Kohn, both for organizing the terrific workshop at the University of Toronto that launched this special issue and for her extremely valuable insights on my own work. I am grateful to all the workshop participants for their comments and critiques, and would like to extend special thanks to Avigail Ferdman for all of her efforts in organizing.

Disclosure statement

No potential conflict of interest was reported by the author.

References

Anderson, B. (1983/2006). *Imagined communities: Reflections on the origin and spread of nationalism*. London: Verso.

Arendt, H. (1951/1994). *The Origins of totalitarianism*. New York, NY: Harcourt.

Aristotle. (1996). *The politics*. In S. Everson (Ed.), B. Jowett (Trans.). Cambridge: Cambridge University Press.

Berger, P. (1969). *The sacred canopy*. Garden City, NY: Anchor Books.

Crepaz, M. (2008). *Trust beyond borders: Immigration, the welfare state, and identity in modern societies*. Ann Arbor: University of Michigan Press.

Durkheim, É. (1912/1995). *The elementary forms of religious life*. (K. E. Fields, Trans.). New York, NY: Free Press.

Ferdman, A. (this issue). Why the intrinsic value of public goods matters.

Gans, C. (2003). *The limits of nationalism*. Cambridge: Cambridge University Press.

Genov, N. (2013). Challenges of individualisation. *International Social Science Journal, 64*, 197–209.

Glover, J. (2012). *Humanity: A moral history of the twentieth century*. New Haven, CT: Yale University Press.

Goffman, E. (1959). *The presentation of self in everyday life*. New York, NY: Doubleday Anchor Books.

Habermas, J. (1992/1998). *Between facts and norms: Contributions to a discourse theory of law and democracy*. (W. Rehg, Trans.). Cambridge: MIT Press.

Habermas, J. (2009). *Europe: The faltering project*. Malden: Polity Press.

Habermas, J., 2012. *The crisis of the European Union*. (C. Cronin, Trans.). Malden: Polity.

Horkheimer, M., & Adorno T. W. (1947/2002). *Dialectic of enlightenment: Philosophical fragments*. In G. S. Noerr (Eds.), E. Jephcott, Trans.). Stanford: Stanford University Press.

Hussain, W. (this issue). Why should we care about competition?

Kant, I. (1784/2008). *Idea for a universal history with a cosmopolitan purpose*. In H. S. Reiss (Ed.), H. B. Nisbet (Trans.). Kant: Political writings (pp. 41–53). Cambridge: Cambridge University Press.

Kant, I. (1790/2000). *Critique of the power of judgment*. In P. Guyer (Ed.), P. Guyer & E. Matthews (Trans.). Cambridge: Cambridge University Press.

Kant, I. (1793/2004). *Religion within the boundaries of mere reason*. (A. Wood & G. D. Giovanni, Ed. and Trans.). Cambridge: Cambridge University Press.

Kohn, M. (this issue). Solidarism and social rights.

Kolers, A. (this issue). Solidarity as environmental justice in brownfields remediation.

SOLIDARITY AND PUBLIC GOODS

Kymlicka, W. (2001). *Politics in the vernacular: Nationalism, multiculturalism, and citizenship.* Oxford: Oxford University Press.

Levinas, E. (1961/1969). *Totality and infinity: An essay on exteriority.* (A. Lingis, Trans.). Pittsburgh, PA: Duquesne University Press.

Levinas, E. (1974/2002). *Otherwise than being, or beyond essence.* (A. Lingis, Trans.). Pittsburgh, PA: Duquesne University Press.

Marin, M. (this issue). Racial structural solidarity.

Miller, D. (1995). *On nationality.* Oxford: Oxford University Press.

Müller, J.-W. (2007). *Constitutional patriotism.* Princeton: Princeton University Press.

Nussbaum, M. 2013. *Political emotions: Why love matters for justice.*

Otto, R. (1917/1958). *The idea of the holy.* (J. W. Harvey, Trans.). New York, NY: Oxford University Press.

Polanyi, K. (1944/2001). *The great transformation: The political and economic origins of our time.* Boston, MA: Beacon Press.

Rawls, J. (1993/2005). *Political liberalism.* New York, NY: Columbia University Press.

Rousseau, J.-J. (1752/2010). *Preface to narcissus.* In V. Gourevitch (Ed. and Trans.), The Discourses and other early political writings (pp. 92–106). Cambridge: Cambridge University Press.

Rousseau, J.-J. (1754/2010). *Discourse on the origin and foundations of inequality among men or second discourse.* In V. Gourevitch (Ed. and Trans.). The discourses and other early political writings (pp. 111–222). Cambridge: Cambridge University Press.

Rousseau, J.-J. (1762/1979). *Emile, or on education.* (A. Bloom, Ed. and Trans.). New York, NY: Basic Books.

Schaeffer, M. (2014). *Ethnic diversity and social cohesion: Immigration, ethnic fractionalization, and potentials for civic action.* Farnham: Ashgate.

Shklar, J. (1984). *Ordinary vices.* Cambridge: Harvard University Press.

Stilz, A. (2009). *Liberal loyalty.* Princeton: Princeton University Press.

Tamir, Y. (1993). *Liberal nationalism.* Princeton: Princeton University Press.

Thompson, D. F. (2008). Deliberative democratic theory and empirical political science. *Annual Review of Political Science, 11,* 497–520.

Tönnies, F. (1887/1957). *Gemeinschaft und Gesellschaft* [Community and society]. (C. P. Loomis, Ed. and Trans.). New York, NY: Harper Torchbooks.

Van der Meer, T., & Tolsma, J. (2014). Ethnic diversity and its supposed detrimental effects on social cohesion. *Annual Review of Sociology, 40,* 459–478.

Weber, M. (1921/1978). *Economy and society.* G. Roth & C. Wittich (Eds.), E. Fischoff, Hans Gerth, C. Wright Mills, Ferdinand Kolegar, A. M. Henderson, T. Parsons, Edward Shils, & Max Rheinstein (Trans.). Berkeley, CA: University of California Press.

Yack, B. (2012). *Nationalism and the moral psychology of community.* Chicago, IL: The University of Chicago Press.

Solidarity and social rights

Margaret Kohn

ABSTRACT
The paper argues that the liberal approach to social rights is contradictory and provides an alternative account that draws on solidarism, a strand of nineteenth-century French Republican thought. Solidarism links together a normative theory of social obligation and a descriptive account of social value, debt and unearned increment. The theory of social property provides a distinctive foundation for social rights.

The International Covenant on Economic, Social, and Cultural rights was adopted in 1966. Article 11 recognizes 'the right of everyone to an adequate standard of living for himself and his family, including adequate food, clothing and housing, and to the continuous improvement of living conditions'. By 1986, 87 countries had formally accepted the related obligations (Alston & Quinn, 1987). The rights to land, housing, food/water and development are among the 'social and economic' rights that are least likely to be constitutionalized. A recent study of 122 constitutions in the developing world, found that economic and social rights are given equal status with civil and political rights in about one third of constitutions (Jung & Rosevear, 2011). Even in places like South Africa and India where social rights have been recognized by the courts, there is a lag between theory and practice.

Social rights are also controversial in wealthy countries. The United States has insisted that social and economic rights are best understood as policy goals rather than justiciable rights. In Canada, activists have argued that the right to life in the Canadian Charter of Rights and Freedoms entails a right to adequate housing. In British Columbia, the Court of Appeal agreed with a version of this argument, but the Ontario Court of Appeal rejected a similar claim.

Courts have been reluctant to recognize social rights because such rights have a distinctive justification. The confusion about these rights is at least partially due to a tension within liberal theory itself. In 'On the Jewish Question', Marx famously pointed out that the paradigmatic right is the right to private property, which prioritizes individual self-interest above social needs. Contemporary theorists have tried to rework liberalism to justify social rights, but this is difficult without an adequate account of the social. In this article, I introduce a strand of radical republicanism called 'solidarism'. Solidarism has a sophisticated account of the social, which enables us to address and overcome the liberal ambivalence about social rights.

The ambivalence within liberal theory can be traced back to the tension between social structure and individual right in the writing of Kant. According to Kant, to be human is to be a rational, purposive agent and the moral force of political authority comes from the way it protects a sphere of freedom. Rational agents must create and submit to political authority because a common judge is the precondition of right and progress. The state is necessary in order to ensure that individuals are not subject to arbitrary domination (Ellis, 2005; Kant, 1991). This approach can justify positive duties, and indeed Kant argues that the sovereign can impose compulsory taxes in order to preserve the poor, e.g. 'those members of society who cannot do so themselves'. (Kant, 1991, p. 149) At the same, however, he notes that extreme material inequality and the resulting relations of dependence are not matters of right that can legitimately be changed through state action (Kant, 1991). According to Kant, equality only requires that the individual's position reflects his talents, efforts or circumstances, rather than 'the irresistible will of any outside party'. (Kant, 1991, p. 77) This passage is significant because it helps us see what is missing in the classic articulation of the liberal approach: an adequate account of circumstances, or social structure.

The normative significance of freedom changes when we recognize that an apparently legitimate exercise of freedom – and not just arbitrary domination – can negatively impact another person's circumstances. The social is a way of describing this interdependence. In the nineteenth century, the concept of 'the social' was also used to explain why individuals had duties to others that took precedence over their private interests. Socialists argued that the right to private property secured freedom for some but generated un-freedom for others. The modern concept of the social emerges in the late nineteenth century in conjunction with urbanization and industrialization. It was both a normative and descriptive concept. According to the theory of solidarism, once people recognize that they are interconnected through cities and sewers, disease and culture, production and consumption, then they will see that both problems and solutions have a social dimension.

In this article, I contrast the liberal and solidarist approach to social rights, but of course these are ideal types. Liberalism, solidarism and even socialism are best understood as complex political ideologies that share commitments to equality and freedom but differ about the meaning and priority of these values and the feasibility of realizing them. The intellectual history of the early twentieth century is filled with fascinating but largely forgotten hybrids (Cunliffe

& Erreygers, 2003). For example, in his book *The New Liberalism: The Ideology of Social Reform* Michael Freeden (1978) describes the social liberalism of TH Green, Hobson, and Hobhouse as a coherent ideology that connected moral obligation, social relationships, and positivist science. Even though social liberalism has largely disappeared as a political discourse, new hybrids such as socialist luck-egalitarianism (Cohen) and left-libertarianism (van Parijs) have emerged in political philosophy. Rutger Claassen (this volume) is right that solidarism is best understood as a form of egalitarianism rather than an alternative to it, but it is distinctive in its diagnostic and political orientation (Sluga, 2014). Solidarism developed out of an earlier critique of ideal theory: the late nineteenth-century critique of Kant. Republican philosophers in France were not satisfied with abstract theories that identified universal duties. They wanted to understand the forces preventing social change, to address the problem of moral and political motivation, and to justify institutional remedies. Solidarism provided a way to do this. The first part of this paper provides a brief intellectual history of solidarism. In the second part, I turn to the liberal justification of social right and highlight some problematic implications of the central role the concept of autonomy plays. In the final section, I consider whether there are ways of reconciling these two approaches.

Social property and solidarism

Solidarism was a strand of radical republicanism that was influential in the late nineteenth and early twentieth centuries in France. The solidarists advanced the concept of social debt as an alternative to the liberal defence of private property rights and the socialist call for the abolition of capitalism. The distinctive critique of both laissez-faire liberalism and socialism was a reorientation of republican thought (Pettit, 1999; Scott, 1951). An earlier generation of French republicans like the philosopher Charles Renouvier thought private property was a guarantee against exploitation, economic domination or enslavement by others. He defined property as 'an instrument of defence against social injustice', and insisted that property was necessary to secure one's aims without having to depend on others (Renouvier, 1872, p. 293). Given this emphasis on private property, republicans were worried that socialism, if it took the form of state control of the economy, would threaten freedom. At the same time, they recognized that the fanatic defence of private property by liberals had become a tool for securing the economic domination of the propertyless. In the late nineteenth century, radical republicans began to realize that changing material conditions forced a rethinking of the concept of property. In industrial society, the ideal of economic independence based on the ownership of land or tools had become obsolete. The solidarists tried to find an alternative to private property, one suited to the modern world and able to serve the critical function of securing independence and mitigating vulnerability to exploitation. It is this feature – the capacity to limit the arbitrary power of the employer – that Jacques Donzelot identifies as the key contribution of the concept of social right: 'It is precisely the support given to disciplinary norms and the employer's power by the particular characteristics of every production that *social right* will break up ….' (Donzelot, 1988) For Donzelot, social right was not about securing subsistence but increasing the power of workers.

In the late nineteenth century, thinkers across the political spectrum were concerned with 'the social question'. The basic challenge was to find a way to address the fact that the massive increase in prosperity brought about through industrialization and trade did not benefit the poor and working classes. Urbanization made social ills more apparent to those who suffered from them and to those who would have preferred to ignore them. Socialists called for revolution and rejected collaboration with the state, which they saw as an instrument of the capitalist class (Stone, 1985). In the mid-nineteenth century, reformers and workers associations experimented with mutual aid societies and cooperatives, but these failed to realize their promise. Mutualism basically involved pooling risk among poor workers who had few resources to pool and cooperatives were underfunded and struggled to compete with well-financed capitalist firms (Donzelot, 1988). In response to these difficulties, the radical republicans began to rethink the role of state as the guarantor of social rights (Bouglé, 1904).

According to the solidarists, the modern division of labour produces a social product (Gide, Rist, & Smart, 1943). If this fact is taken seriously, the theoretical rationale for private property becomes untenable. The philosophical foundation of solidarism was a critique of the Lockean theory of private property. The solidarist philosopher Alfred Fouillée criticized the laissez-faire school on the grounds that it rested on a distorted account property. According to Fouillée, only the God of Genesis created something out of nothing. Humans produce useful things by shaping and forming to material objects such as land, stone or wood. By refining existing technologies, subsequent generations become more adept at reshaping the world (Fouillée, 1885). Fouillée argued that it is an error to conceive of private property as a *right* given that the legitimate claim to the product of one's labour does not encompass a claim to the material mixed with labour. This error stems from the problematic starting point of 'the state of nature'. When, following Locke, philosophers imagine a state of nature without scarcity, they treat the value of materials as low and the value of labour as high and therefore assign the entire value of the product to the labour. In actual societies, however, materials are scarce and labour is socialized therefore the product is social rather than private property.

The solidarists justified economic redistribution by building on this premise and reworking arguments from law and political economy. I want to draw attention to the key concepts of debt and rent. According to the solidarists, a large portion of private property is actually social value inherited from past generations and created through the division of labour and therefore 'every man owes either his forebears or his contemporaries the best part of what he has, and even of what he is'. (Gide, Rist, and Smart 1943). For Léon Bourgeois, the leader of the Radical Republican Party, the way to discharge this debt was for those who command too large a share of the social product to redistribute it to those who have too little. The solidarist concept of rent builds on Ricardo's insight that the revenue accrued to the owner of land may vary, even if the same amount of labour and capital is applied to the same amount of land. Ricardo called the difference between the two yields 'unearned increment'. In economically developed societies, the difference is usually not caused by the natural features of the land but rather the presence of social factors such as the rule of law, markets, infrastructure, transportation, etc. According to solidarists, *earned* increment should go to the individual and *rent* should be allocated to and by society (Kohn, 2016a).

The theory of solidarism links together a normative theory of social obligation and a descriptive account of social value. While solidarism as a comprehensive political ideology has lost influence, the theory of social rights has had an after-life in normative political thought (Alperovitz, 2008; Van Parijs, 1991) Some features of this theory resemble what Alan Gewirth called the 'world ownership' thesis. The 'world ownership thesis', holds that the world was originally held in common, therefore no one can claim exclusive ownership of any part of it by virtue of his labour (Gewirth, 1998). The structure of the argument goes like this: since A produces X with the help of Y, which is owned by H (all humans or all the members of A's society), then X is at least partially owned by H (Gewirth, 1998). There are two versions of this argument. The strong version concludes that A holds no ownership rights over Y. The weaker version holds that H and A have some kind of shared ownership of X (Cohen, 1986). The latter is the solidarist view. It recognizes that A has made a special contribution to the production of X, which justifies a partial claim upon it. I will describe this as 'the social property thesis' since this label better captures the distinctive features of the approach.

The social property thesis provides a distinctive foundation for social rights. If the world was originally held in common, then all people have a common or social property right. This right has priority over the individual interest in the unlimited accumulation of wealth. This approach differs from the liberal theory of social rights; while the underlying goal of human flourishing is similar, the solidarist social theory helps us see that the benefits of interdependence imply corresponding responsibilities. Both the liberal and the solidarist approaches share a concern with a decent life, which includes material well-being (food, shelter, medical care) and opportunity (education). For the solidarists, however, the corresponding duty rests with society, and, in modern times, this means the state, which has a fiduciary responsibility to protect the interests of citizens (Fox-Decent, 2005). Being a member of society is like being a stock holder of a joint stock company and each person has a claim on dividends as an heir to a shared inheritance. This means that meeting social needs does not require taking one person's property and giving it to another; it involves distributing the social surplus (Van Parijs, 1991). But, if social right is not simply the aggregate of individual entitlements, then what is it? The content of social right will reflect cultural values, level of economic development, and democratic deliberation, but at a minimum it implies three things: a limit on individual appropriation (a negative desert argument); a guarantee of subsistence; and an ethos of solidarity.

The liberal approach to social rights

In what follows, I use the label 'liberal approach' to describe the subset of liberal theories that emphasize ontological individualism and universal well-being (Rawls, 2001). By ontological individualism, I mean that the starting point is the autonomous individual who reflects about the principles that would secure his or her autonomy in a world shared with people who have their own interests, desires and values. Rawls's original position is a vivid and powerful illustration of this worldview, but less abstract approaches share the same premises. Citizens of liberal societies and students of political philosophy are taught to ask the following question: given that others have the same rights as I do, how do we arrange things so that I can achieve my purposes and they can achieve theirs? It is hard to even recognize that this is a distinctive point of view rather than an uncontroversial starting point, but one could begin with something quite different. For example, we could ask, 'Given that I was born utterly helpless, and my sustenance and survival depended entirely on the care provided - and indeed the world created - by others, what do I owe to them?'

The liberal approach begins with the equal claim to a decent life and emphasizes that such a life involves both autonomy and well-being (Fabre, 2000). Autonomy protects the ability to pursue the good life and for liberals this means the life that is good from my point of view. This does not necessarily imply selfishness since it could involve a life devoted to service to others or to religious devotion. The second dimension, well-being, consists in the abilities and conditions that are required for acting at all (Gewirth, 1998, p. 14). Well-being is the capacity necessary to do things in the world.

In *Social Rights under the Constitution*, Cecile Fabre argues that the interest in well-being implies a right to a minimally decent standard of living. Notwithstanding some technical differences, Fabre's core argument in favour of social rights is similar to the one in Henry Shue's path-breaking book *Basic Rights* (Shue, 1996). In order to secure autonomy and well-being, individuals' material needs must be guaranteed. Rights are instruments that protect 'fundamental interests' and the prevention of physical suffering from hunger, exposure, and ill health are among our most overwhelming interests. The logic of the argument is straightforward. Individuals have a fundamental interest in a decent life and if their needs are not met, then a decent life is impossible.

To describe something as a right implies a corresponding duty (Hohfeld, 1913). It is this component of the argument, however, that generates difficulties for the liberal approach. The liberal approach rests on the view the individuals are autonomous agents who are primarily responsible for themselves. Alan Gewirth calls this the theory of 'productive agency' (Gewirth, 1998). Autonomy means that individuals set their own ends and pursue their own understanding of the good. To do so, individuals must have certain capacities and also opportunities to live the kind of life that they want for themselves. Liberal theorists emphasize that in order to exercise autonomy, individuals must have subjective capacities such as judgement and material resources to carry out their purposes (Raz, 1986).

Who is responsible for providing the things necessary for a minimally decent life? It could be the individual, everyone, some subset of individuals such as the family, or a designated institution such as the state. Fabre criticizes approaches that assign exclusive responsibility to the political community. I will examine these arguments below. The upshot of these critiques, however, is the conclusion that social rights are universal and therefore the state, other institutions, and even private actors must try to ensure the well-being of everyone. The logic is that a right implies an obligation and, barring some principled way to limit its scope, the obligation must be general. But this opens up a potentially unlimited scope of obligation. Even if we concede that basic material needs are not literally unlimited, they are quite extensive. There are plenty of things that are fundamental to our well-being that cannot take the form for rights, for example love, social ties, and respect. An individual may need love but does not have a right to love. Is the interest in autonomy/well-being more like the need for love or more like the right to a fair trial?

To answer this question we must take a step back and try to reconstruct the assumptions underlying the liberal approach to social rights. The concept of autonomy plays an important role in the liberal tradition and is connected to moral and legal responsibility (Fischer & Ravizza, 1999; Ripstein, 1998). Because individuals are able to select which goals to pursue, they are also responsible for the outcomes of their intentional actions. According to Christine Korsgaard, from the Kantian perspective, 'To hold someone responsible is to regard her as a *person* – that is to say, as a free and equal person capable of acting both rationally and morally' (Korsgaard, 1992). This implies that the person who is primarily responsible for the agent's well-being is the person herself.

Personal responsibility has always played an important role in discussions of welfare rights because of the nature of the need being met. Other constitutional positive rights have a different structure; they protect things that no individual can provide for himself. Take, for example, the right to vote or the right to a fair trial. The individual cannot secure these things for him or herself. A formal institutional structure is necessary to guarantee these rights. Most people can secure shelter and food through a combination of the following:

their own labour, voluntary market exchange, or access to resources pooled among family members.

Of course there are circumstances under which people cannot provide for themselves. A key idea that runs through left-liberal theory is that individuals are responsible for the consequences of their choices but not the circumstances that are beyond their control. This is called luck egalitarianism. While there are extensive debates about exactly what this means in practice, the central idea is that justice would take the form of a generous insurance scheme that ensures that the distribution of valued things does not depend on luck (Anderson, 1999; Arneson, 2004; Barry, 2006; Scheffler, 2003; Segall, 2007).

If we apply this principle to social rights, we would conclude that individuals are responsible for their own well-being, except when they are unable to do so due to circumstances beyond their control. I will bracket for a second the question of who should help out, and focus on another problem. How can we tell which circumstances are beyond the individual's control? In debates that take place at the level of ideal theory, this can, perhaps, be dismissed as unimportant, but if social rights are intended to inform public policy and the corresponding legal obligations are to be imposed by courts, then this question cannot be ignored. The distinction between the wilful and the unlucky is basically the distinction between the deserving and underserving poor. How can we differentiate between Mary (a person who worked extremely hard but due to modest abilities became a low-wage worker and was laid off due to de-industrialization) and Jane (a person with keen intelligence and social privilege, who partied throughout college and young adulthood, struggled to hold a job, and ended up a low-wage worker and was laid off due to the restructuring of the retail sector)? We may be able to draw a moral distinction between these two cases, but not a legal one or practical one. Even the most intrusive, paternalistic and disciplinary welfare bureaucracy cannot distinguish between them.

It is possible to respond to this objection with a shrug of the shoulders. Perhaps it simply doesn't matter whether someone is responsible for the fact they are unable to fulfil their own needs. Or alternately, we might just accept that in order to fulfil our legitimate obligation to Mary, Jane will also benefit (Goodin, 1988). But this example shows why the liberal approach tends to favour the welfare-as-safety net approach to well-being. If people are responsible for their choices and the outcomes of those choices, then social 'rights' will primarily take the form of equal opportunity (comprehensive public education) and means-tested benefits.

This is better than no safety net at all, but it falls short of the promise of the concept of social rights. Unlike say the rights to free speech or free exercise of religion, which are granted to all people by virtue of their humanity, these residual welfare rights are granted to people who are unable to successfully function as 'productive agents' (Gewirth, 1998). The social obligation only extends to people whose inability is no fault of their own, and given the difficulty of distinguishing between those who are entitled and those who aren't entitled, this approach results in a paternalistic state that tries to shape the behaviour of beneficiaries through rewards and punishments. Potentially intrusive forms of surveillance and monitoring are necessary to ensure that only the unlucky and not the dissolute are the beneficiaries of the state's residual obligation to secure social rights (Cruikshank, 1999; Smith, 2007; Soss, Fording, & Schram, 2011). While it is true that the state ultimately decides on the acceptable limits of all rights, including classic civil rights such as freedom of speech, here the discretion of the state takes a different form. In cases dealing with civil rights, the question is whether the rights of the individual threaten the public good or the rights of others. In conflicts over welfare rights, the question, at least implicitly, is different, since only the unlucky are legitimate holders of a claim against the state.

Critiques and comparisons

While there are theoretical differences between solidarist social property and liberal autonomy, there have also been influential attempts to combine them. Philippe van Parijs's case for a basic income rests on solidarist ideas about social property (Van Parijs, 1991, 2004) Van Parijs suggests that a basic income would maximize freedom by enabling a real choice of how to live. The social property thesis is used to refute the objection that the freedom of some would result in the coercion of others who would have to pay taxes to support other people's less productive lifestyle choices. This is convincing, but in van Parijs's formulation, the social property thesis is subordinated to a normative principle that is conceptually unrelated and possibly even antithetical: the primacy of individual freedom. Social property could be distributed to individuals, but it could also be allocated to collective consumption or fostering spiritual life, as Europeans did in the Middle Ages. The solidarists shared van Parijs's concern with freedom, but they interpreted it somewhat differently. They weren't left libertarians and their goal wasn't to maximize individual freedom but rather to address the fact that economic structures made the freedom of some rest on the exploitation of others. They also wanted to shelter people from the new forms of dependence that were emerging, and to do so without unleashing violent class conflict. In order to achieve these goals, the solidarists tried to combine distribution to the needy with another dimension of social right, one that has been largely forgotten today: bargaining power. The solidarists worried about a new and potentially despotic form of power in the factory, and advocated regulations which could increase the bargaining power of workers (Donzelot, 1988). To temper this agonistic side of their programme, they also promoted public schools and other public spaces that reinforced the ethos of solidarity (Connolly, 2010, 2013).

The problem with the libertarian variant of the social property thesis is apparent when viewed from the perspective of politics rather than ideal theory. If freedom is placed above solidarity, then it becomes difficult to accept, or even recognize, social obligations. Recall the derisive reaction to Obama's speech telling business owners 'you didn't build that' (all by yourselves). The angry response was the product of a neoliberal ideology that succeeded at cultivating an ethos of individualism. It is difficult to believe in the existence of social property and to accept the corresponding obligations, when subjects are formed through individualizing practices and a language of choice, self and autonomy.

This is where the *social* theory of social rights parts ways with the liberal approach and the difference relates to the second theme of the volume: public goods. From a solidarist perspective, public goods, in the normative sense of the term, are not the ones that the market cannot supply efficiently. Nor are they justified by a perfectionist theory of higher goods. They are justified in a consequentialist manner; public goods are the forms of collective consumption and experience that make it possible to imagine ourselves as connected to one another. They are legitimate in so far as they help solve the notorious problem of moral motivation: why do people decide to do things that are not in their immediate self-interest? Why should the privileged, in their role as democratic citizens, bind themselves to a legal obligation to pay their social debts? A rich public life can foster an ethos of solidarity by connecting the self and the social world.

The concept of solidarity has also been subject to critique. Solidarity is linked to national identity (Miller, 1979, 1995) or community belonging and critics argue that such theories take the contingent and morally arbitrary fact of shared proximity or history and treat it as a criterion for fulfilling or abrogating our general duties. Does this critique apply to the social property thesis? Yes and No. In conjunction with other arguments, the social property thesis can be applied to different scales of justice: global, national or local. Social rights, however, involve both a theory and an institutional practice. Social rights are legal rights that are recognized by courts, which have the authority to compel the state to enact or modify policies to secure these rights. In other words, the practice of social rights assumes the existing institutional structure of states. In keeping with the method of diagnostic theory, which focuses on concrete choices and judgements rather than abstract problems, I see this reconstruction of solidarist theory as a contribution to debates in places like Canada where there is a discussion about whether to recognize social rights (Sluga, 2014).

This pragmatic response, however, is only partially satisfying because it evades the important question whether national identity and communal bonds are the moral basis of obligation. A full response to this question would require a separate essay, but I will briefly introduce the main claims here. First, solidarism emphasizes interdependence, proximity, and division of labour, and concludes that these social facts do have moral significance. According to the solidarists, there are associative duties that are non-contractual obligations derived from relationships (Kolodny, 2002; Lazar, 2009). The solidarists insisted that the rich and poor are, in fact, part of a cooperative venture, one that generates aggregate prosperity and a corresponding obligation to structure cooperation to ensure mutual benefit. Second, solidarism is meant to inform democratic deliberation not to replace it. The best way to allocate social value cannot be determined through empirical science or abstract reason alone, therefore courts and legislatures will have to make judgements about priorities and trade-offs. Third, the moral significance of membership is not exhausted by the way it does or doesn't justify particular obligations. Solidarity is also a source of identity and ethical motivation.

In *Social Rights under the Constitution*, Cecile Fabre points out that the social cooperation account is basically a 'compensatory justice' argument. This position holds that since members of a community cooperate to build the fabric of society and to accumulate social wealth, if some do not get their fair share, they are owed compensation (Fabre, 2000). For example, blacks in the United States are owed compensation for slavery and Jim Crow, institutions which systematically allocated social wealth in unfair ways (Mills, 2013; Pateman & Mills, 2007). From the solidarist perspective, this is a more extreme version of what happens in the market. Workers, who have little bargaining power, are harmed by a system that generates wealth that benefits others. The beneficiaries of social production should compensate those who do not benefit. From this perspective, distributive justice is a form of compensatory justice.

Fabre notes two problems with this line of argument. The indeterminacy critique emphasizes that it is impossible to know what people contributed and what they are owed. This is correct, but similar concerns arise when putting other theories into practice. For example, need-based welfare programmes are not really tailored to a person's needs but instead provide a standardized level of benefits which are generous for some people and inadequate for others. The needs of the individual are not standard. They vary based on the cost-of-living, tastes, and the existence of other in-kind supports. If social rights are expanded to include autonomy, as Fabre thinks they must be, then it becomes even more difficult to identify a standard benefit that could secure this capacity.

The more serious problem with a compensatory approach is the mismatch between what people need and what they are owed. A disabled person may make no contribution to social property, but meeting his needs is extremely costly. This example is not an exception but an illustration of a general problem. According to critics of the compensation approach, the purpose of social rights is not to restore the *status quo ante* bur rather to create a more just situation (Goodin, 1988). Furthermore, the social right to education is forward looking and therefore does not fit well with a theory of compensation.

These objections may apply to a pure theory of compensatory justice, but they do not apply to the 'social property thesis'. According to the social property thesis, *individuals* are not being compensated for something akin to wage theft. Surplus value is owed to society and it provides the resources necessary to fund social rights. It is not a theory of individual desert but rather what Robert Goodin called a negative desert claim (Goodin, 1985).

It is a way of explaining why individuals do not necessarily deserve their wealth and are not morally entitled to monopolize it for their own benefit. Viewed in this way, it is a way of supporting, reinforcing, and realizing other theories of structural justice and redistribution.

The key concept is rent rather than surplus value. The social value attached to urban property was a favourite example of the solidarists. If a man purchases a plot on the island of Manhattan in 1770 and his grandson sells the plot for 50 times its original cost, the beneficiary's wealth is not the result of purposive labour. The increase in value was produced entirely by the community, which, in the intervening years, transformed a remote outpost into a bustling hub of commerce. The normative idea is not that we must give the individual what she is owed but that we must use social wealth to promote the flourishing of all members of society. It is a way of making good on the Lockean proviso that 'as much and as good' must be guaranteed to those whose birthright – the commons – was taken. It is precisely because a return to the status quo ante is not possible, that this alternative is necessary.

Conclusion

This article has shown the limitations of the liberal theory of social rights. The key features of the liberal approach – autonomy, luck and responsibility – only generate a very limited obligation to protect the bare life of the unlucky. So far, I have argued that the liberal approach provides a cogent account of a residualist, disciplinary welfare state, but it does not provide a convincing justification of social rights. This is due to the tension in liberal theory between the ideal of individual freedom, which implies a limited state, and the ideal of equality, which requires an expansive one. We can see this tension in the reluctance of courts to constitutionalize social rights (Kohn, 2016b). The underlying logic is the Kantian one: courts can provide a remedy for acts of arbitrary domination but not for circumstances. The tension exists in solidarism too, but by introducing the third term, fraternity or solidarity, the case for equality is strengthened.

In conclusion, I would like to respond briefly to some objections to the analysis presented above. The first objection is that the welfare state does not reassemble the picture that I have painted; in both theory and practice, it is based on universal entitlements rather than desert and discretion (Esping-Andersen, 1990). It is true that actual welfare regimes and programs take a range of different forms that reflect the political coalitions, social movements and ideologies that influenced their formation. Welfare regimes often include both solidarist and liberal–paternalist components. My goal has been to show that there is a theoretical reason that liberal welfare states often emphasize means-tested programmes. The language of solidarity could also be employed to justify means tested or paternalist programmes, but there are good reasons why this would be much more difficult (Béland, 2009; Béland & Hansen, 2000). The structural analysis of the benefits and burdens of cooperation shows that neither our accomplishments nor our vulnerabilities are fully our own. The social property thesis is an alternative to common sense assumptions about 'desert' and re-describes social right as a claim to a shared inheritance.

The second objection is that solidarism actually differs very little from left-liberal theories of justice. The Rawlsian original position could be read as an attempt to de-naturalize private property. Behind the veil of ignorance, individuals are asked to decide on principles of justice and the second principle, the difference principle, holds that inequalities should benefit the least well off. This could be interpreted in two different ways. One possibility is that wealth and income are seen as naturally belonging to individuals who are obliged to support just institutions that secure redistribution. The second possibility is that we imagine a state of nature with common property and create institutions exist to secure a fair distribution among individuals and between public and private shares. Rawls was usually understood as intending the former, and even the suggestive remarks on property owning democracy do not fully endorse the latter (Rawls, 2001) but solidarism makes it possible to see Rawls' theory in a new way.

While there are potential areas of overlap between the liberal and solidarist approaches, there are also differences. A social theory of social rights rests on a different way of viewing the person. People are born vulnerable and dependent. Social ties sustain us, and therefore we should repair and strengthen them. Social cooperation generates more than the sum of its parts, but as Rousseau warned, once there is a surplus, some will take too much leaving others with too little. The concept of social right is like the binding of Ulysses; a way of committing ourselves to pay our social debts. This commitment stems more from our precarity than our autonomy. Once we realize that the human condition is interdependence and vulnerability (Butler, 2015), we can recognize that social rights are a way to minimize precarity.

Disclosure statement

No potential conflict of interest was reported by the author.

References

Alperovitz, G. (2008). *Unjust deserts: How the rich are taking our common inheritance.* New York, NY: New Press.

Alston, P., & Quinn, G. (1987). The nature and scope of states parties' obligations under the international covenant on economic, social and cultural rights. *Human Rights Quarterly, 9*(2), 156–229.

Anderson, E. S. (1999). What is the point of equality? *Ethics, 109*(2), 287–337.

Arneson, R. J. (2004). Luck egalitarianism interpreted and defended. *Philosophical Topics, 32*(1/2), 1–20.

Barry, N. (2006). Defending luck egalitarianism. *Journal of Applied Philosophy, 23*(1), 89–107.

Béland, D. (2009). Back to bourgeois? French social policy and the idea of solidarity. *International Journal of Sociology and Social Policy, 29*(9/10), 445–456.

Béland, D., & Hansen, R. (2000). Reforming the French welfare state: Solidarity, social exclusion and the three crises of citizenship. *West European Politics, 23*(1), 47–64.

Bouglé, C. (1904). *Le Solidarisme.* Paris: Edourd Cornely. Solidarisme et Liberalisme.

Butler, J. (2015). *Notes toward a performative theory of assembly.* Cambridge, MA: Harvard University Press.

Claassen, R. (This volume). Justice as a claim to (social) property.

Cohen, G. A. (1986). Self-ownership, world ownership, and equality: Part II. *Social Philosophy and Policy, 3*(2), 77–96.

Connolly, W. E. (2010). *A World of becoming.* Durham, NC: Duke University Press.

Connolly, W. E. (2013). *The fragility of things: Self-organizing processes, neoliberal fantasies, and democratic activism.* Durham, NC: Duke University Press.

Cruikshank, B. (1999). *The will to empower: Democratic citizens and other subjects.* Ithaca, NY: Cornell University Press.

Cunliffe, J., & Erreygers, G. (2003). 'Basic income? Basic capital!' origins and issues of a debate. *Journal of Political Philosophy, 11*(1), 89–110.

Donzelot, J. (1988). The promotion of the social. *Economy and Society, 17*(3), 395–427.

Ellis, E. (2005). *Kant's Politics: Provisional Theory for an Uncertain World.* New Haven, CT: Yale University Press.

Esping-Andersen, G. (1990). *The three worlds of welfare capitalism.* Princeton, NJ: Princeton University Press.

Fabre, C. (2000). *Social rights under the constitution: Government and the decent life.* Oxford: Oxford University Press.

Fischer, J. M., & Ravizza, M. (1999). *Responsibility and control: A theory of moral responsibility.* (1st ed.). Cambridge: Cambridge University Press.

Fouillée, A. (1885). *La science sociale contemporaine.* Paris: Hachette et cie.

Fox-Decent, E. (2005). The fiduciary nature of state legal authority. *Queen's Law Journal, 31*, 259–310.

Freeden, M. (1978). *The New Liberalism: An Ideology of Social Reform.* Oxford: Clarendon Press.

Gewirth, A. R. (1998). *The community of rights.* Springer.

Gide, C., Rist, C., & Smart, W. (1943). *Economic doctrines, a history of.* London: G.G. Harrap & Company.

Goodin, R. E. (1985). Negating positive desert claims. *Political Theory, 13*(4), 575–598.

Goodin, R. E. (1988). *Reasons for welfare: The political theory of the welfare state*. Princeton, NJ: Princeton University Press.

Hohfeld, W. N. (1913). Some fundamental legal conceptions as applied in judicial reasoning. *The Yale Law Journal, 23*(1), 16–59.

Jung, C., & Rosevear, E. (2011). *Economic and Social Rights in Developing Country Constitutions: Preliminary Report on the TIESR Dataset*. Draft for comment, University of Toronto.

Kant, I. (1991). *Kant: Political writings* (2nd ed.). Cambridge: Cambridge University Press.

Kohn, M. (2016a). The critique of possessive individualism. *Political Theory, 44*(5), 603–628.

Kohn, M. (2016b). *The death and life of the urban commonwealth* (Reprinted.). New York, NY: Oxford University Press.

Kolodny, N. (2002). Do associative duties matter? *Journal of Political Philosophy, 10*(3), 250–266.

Korsgaard, C. M. (1992). Creating the kingdom of ends: Reciprocity and responsibility in personal relations. *Philosophical Perspectives, 6*, 305–332.

Lazar, S. (2009). Debate: Do associative duties really not matter? *Journal of Political Philosophy, 17*(1), 90–101.

Miller, D. (1979). *Social justice*. Oxford: Oxford University Press.

Miller, D. (1995). *On nationality*. Oxford: Clarendon Press.

Mills, C. W. (2013). Retrieving rawls for racial justice? A critique of Tommie Shelby. *Critical Philosophy of Race, 1*(1), 1–27.

Pateman, C., & Mills, C. W. (2007). *Contract and domination*. Cambridge: Polity.

Pettit, P. (1999). *Republicanism: A Theory of Freedom and Government*. Oxford: Oxford University Press. DOI: https://doi.org/10.1093/0198296428.001.0001

Rawls, J. (2001). *Justice as fairness: A restatement* (2nd ed.). Cambridge, MA: Belknap Press of Harvard University Press.

Raz, J. (1986). *The morality of freedom*. Oxford: Clarendon Press.

Renouvier, C. (1872). Du droit personnel de défense. *Critique Philosophique, 2*.

Ripstein, A. (1998). *Equality, responsibility, and the law*. Cambridge: Cambridge University Press.

Scheffler, S. (2003). What is Egalitrianism? *Philosophy & Public Affairs, 31*(1), 5–39.

Scott, J. A. (1951). *Republican ideas and the liberal tradition in France 1870–1914* (1st American ed.). New York, NY: Columbia University Press.

Segall, S. (2007). In solidarity with the imprudent: A defense of luck egalitarianism. *Social Theory and Practice, 33*(2), 177–198.

Shue, H. (1996). *Basic rights: Subsistence, affluence, and US foreign policy*. Princeton, NJ: Princeton University Press.

Sluga, H. (2014). *Politics and the search for the common good*. Cambridge: Cambridge University Press.

Smith, A. M. (2007). *Welfare reform and sexual regulation*. Cambridge: Cambridge University Press.

Soss, J., Fording, R. C., & Schram, S. (2011). *Disciplining the poor: Neoliberal paternalism and the persistent power of race*. Chicago, IL: University of Chicago Press.

Stone, J. F. (1985). *The search for social peace: Reform legislation in France, 1890–1914*. Albany, NY: SUNY Press.

Van Parijs, P. (1991). Why surfers should be fed: The liberal case for an unconditional basic income. *Philosophy & Public Affairs, 20*(2), 101–131.

Van Parijs, P. (2004). Basic income: A simple and powerful idea for the twenty-first century. *Politics & Society, 32*(1), 7–39.

ĝ OPEN ACCESS

Justice as a claim to (social) property

Rutger Claassen

ABSTRACT
Margaret Kohn argues for a reappraisal of early twentieth-century left-republican French political theory, known as 'solidarism'. Solidarism recognises private property as legitimate, but at the same time argues that the collective nature of economic production gives rise to a claim to *social property*. It is social property that should underlie the case for social justice and social rights, not the standard liberal claims to individual autonomy. This paper provides an appraisal of Kohn's recovery of solidarism, taking as its main theme the relation between property and social justice. The paper first offers a typology of four theories of justice (right- and left-libertarianism, luck and relational egalitarianism) and discusses the relation of each of these to the concept of property. Then it argues that solidarism is akin to left-libertarianism in the way it formulates justice as a claim to social property. Finally, it argues that solidarists cannot escape grounding their theory in a non-property based fundamental principle, which makes the theory much less distinctive from egalitarian theories of justice than may appear at first sight.

Introduction

In two recent articles (one of which in this special issue) Margaret Kohn argues for a reappraisal of early twentieth-century left-republican French political theory, known as 'solidarism'. She presents it as charting a middle path between laissez-faire capitalism on the one hand and both welfare state capitalism and socialism on the other hand. Solidarism recognises private property as legitimate, but at the same time argues that the collective nature of economic production gives rise to a claim to *social property*. It is social property that should underlie the case for social justice and social rights, not the standard liberal claims to individual autonomy (Kohn, 2016, this issue).

This is an Open Access article distributed under the terms of the Creative Commons Attribution-NonCommercial-NoDerivatives License (http://creativecommons.org/licenses/by-nc-nd/4.0/), which permits non-commercial re-use, distribution, and reproduction in any medium, provided the original work is properly cited, and is not altered, transformed, or built upon in any way.

This paper provides an appraisal of Kohn's recovery of solidarism, taking as its main theme the relation between property and social justice. Libertarian theories of justice, both in their left-wing and their right-wing variants, build their core principles of justice in terms of a notion of property. Egalitarian theories (as diverse as luck egalitarianism and relational egalitarianism) typically don't make property so central; for them property rights should be defined in a second step, by assessing instrumental considerations about which scheme of property rights best realises their egalitarian principles, which themselves aren't formulated in terms of property rights. I will argue that solidarism is akin to left-libertarianism in the way it formulates justice as a claim to social property. I will also argue that solidarists cannot escape grounding their theory in a non-property based fundamental principle, which makes the theory much less distinctive from egalitarian theories of justice than may appear at first sight.

The first part of the paper offers a conceptual exploration: do current theories of justice make property claims central to justice? I start from a diagnosis of right-wing libertarianism, in which a strong property claim is central. Its moral principle is the defence of self-ownership and free acquisition of property in external goods. Institutionally, this leads to a defence of a purely capitalist economy. The paper then zooms in on three alternative theories of justice: left-libertarianism, luck egalitarianism and relational egalitarianism. These theories make much less use of a notion of property, although there are important differences between them. On this basis, the second part of the paper assesses Kohn's plea for a revival of solidarism. First, I show that solidarism's claim to social property shares structural similarities with left-libertarianism, even if it also diverges from left-libertarianism on some points. Second, I assess the solidarist's criticism of liberal egalitarianism. I argue that on closer inspection solidarism must rely on similar considerations as egalitarians do when it defines the basis of its claim to social property. This basis for solidarists lies in one's membership in a given society, while for egalitarians it lies in a claim to individual autonomy. In both cases, a fundamental non-property based consideration lies at the roots of the claim to a share of social property.

Capitalism, private property and right-libertarianism

Gerald Gaus puts forward the idea that capitalism can be understood as the system of 'maximally extensive property rights', along two dimensions (Gaus, 2010). First, property rights involve a number of different rights: rights to use an object, to exclude others from use, to modify or destroy an object, to sell the object, to earn an income from letting others use the object, etc. Lawyers call these the 'incidents' of ownership, and they consider full private property rights to be given where a person has the full bundle of all incidents of property (Becker, 1977, pp. 18–20; Honoré, 1987). Governments can limit each of these rights. A capitalist society grants as many rights to property owners as possible.

Second, property rights can range over more or less objects. A capitalist economy brings as many objects as possible into the system of private ownership. Here there are key roles for the commodification of natural resources (preventing tragedy of the commons), and the commodification of labour. In addition, all kinds of controversial goods can be brought into the realm of private property (e.g. commodification of body parts).[1] Using these two dimensions, one can plot economic systems by the extent to which they choose to restrict or expand property rights with respect to the bundle of rights and the objects of property (Gaus, 2010).

This scheme needs to be extended. Gaus' two-dimensional definition is symptomatic of a lot of writing in political philosophy, in its focus on property as private property (Christman, 1994; Munzer, 1990; Ryan, 1984; Waldron, 1988). His second dimension conflates the question whether something can become the object of property arrangements (of whatever kind) with the question whether this must be private property. It is one thing to argue that natural resources should be the object of some kind of property arrangement, it is quite another thing to assign this property to the state, a corporation, an individual, etc. Disentangling these two questions, we should recognise *three* dimensions on which to plot economic systems: the subjects of property, the objects of property and the scope of property rights. Capitalism is the system where property is held privately, every object can become property, and the bundle of rights is maximally extensive for the private owner (see Table 1).

Lawyers normally think in terms of an ideal-typical trichotomy of private, common and state property. Private property assigns the power to make decisions about the object to a particular individual, in exclusion to others. Common (or joint) property belongs to a group of people who can all make use of the object, without being able to exclude the other members of the group. Collective (or public/state) property also belongs to a group, but here decisions about the use of the object are made in the interest of the group as a whole. Individual members do not have free access to the object (Dagan & Heller, 2001, pp. 555–558; Lehavi, 2008, p. 139; Waldron, 1988, pp. 38–42). These are ideal types, and different regimes may be chosen for different objects, as will ordinarily be the case in mixed economies. Nonetheless, the ideal types provide organising ideas. Jeremy Waldron even linked preferences for these

Table 1. Dimensions of property.

	Question	Possible answers
(1a) Subjects	Who is allowed to hold property?	Private, common or state property
(1b) Objects	What can become object of a property right?	Controversies include: human beings (slavery), but also human organs (kidneys), ideas (intellectual property), plants, etc.
(1c) Prerogatives	What are owners allowed to do?	A 'bundle of rights': using, selling, managing, etc., one's property

types to distinct political positions: 'To put it crudely: socialists argue for a system of collective property, radicals for something like common property, and capitalists and their liberal ideologues for private property' (Waldron, 1988, p. 44). As we will see, the mapping of normative theories with economic systems is much more problematic than this quote suggests.

Right-libertarianism is the theory of justice that provides the philosophical defence of capitalism, as defined in this three-dimensional space. It does so by making two property claims central. First, right-libertarians invariably defend self-ownership: a person is the owner of his own body, energy, and talents (Mack, 2002; Narveson, 2001; Nozick, 1974). This idea implies a direct rejection of any claims of others upon my body, energy and labour. Self-ownership is widely accepted in so far as others should not be allowed to infringe upon our bodily integrity (through assaults such as rape). For present purposes the more relevant question is whether self-ownership also has consequences for the ownership of our talents and our labour, and from there to ownership of the fruits of our labour (the products we make exerting our talents upon some object). This question inevitably brings in the ownership of material things external to ourselves: self-ownership is a necessary but not sufficient condition for the justification of full private ownership in worldly objects. With respect to these external things, libertarians start from the idea that they are originally either owned in common by all men (e.g. as a gift from God, as in Locke) or unowned. Which of these two points of departure is chosen doesn't really matter – in both cases the libertarian theory defends a transition to individual ownership. Normally this step is defended by arguing that anyone mixing his labour with the resource comes to own it (Locke, 2003; Nozick, 1974).[2]

Taking self-ownership and labour acquisition together gives one the libertarian case for maximally extensive property rights.[3] The concept of property (in the self and external objects) stands at the heart of the libertarian theory of justice and leads more-or-less directly to an institutional defence of capitalism.

In search of solidarity: three alternative theories

This section focuses on three alternative (families of) theories of justice – left-libertarianism, luck egalitarianism and relational egalitarianism – which have become important challengers to right-libertarianism. Each of them can be used to argue in favour of economic schemes that in one sense or the other aim to realise more 'solidarity' than right-libertarian's endorsement of pure capitalism.

Left-libertarianism concurs with right-libertarianism on the question of self-ownership, but diverges from it with respect to world-ownership (Otsuka, 1998; Steiner, 1994; van Parijs, 1995).[4] Individuals may not simply appropriate external resources as much as they can mix their labour with. Instead the ownership of external resources must be divided according to some egalitarian principle. Different variations are possible in terms of the exact principle used for the distribution of external resources, e.g. in terms of strictly equal (or equally valuable) shares, or in terms of joint ownership. Their egalitarian position on world-ownership is due to left-libertarians taking more seriously than right-libertarians the Lockean proviso on the acquisition of resources: individuals can appropriate natural resources only under the condition that 'enough and as good' is left for others. What is enough and as good can differ, but it leads to a more egalitarian distribution of property than right-libertarians would allow.

Luck egalitarianism goes one step further than left-libertarianism in its divergence from right-libertarianism. Luck egalitarians concur with left-libertarians that every individual deserves an equal share of all external resources. For example, in Ronald Dworkin's island thought-experiment, all inhabitants get an equal bundle of clamshells (Dworkin, 2000). However, they diverge from both in their position on self-ownership. Luck egalitarianism – like relational egalitarianism, see hereafter – rejects the idea of self-ownership. Instead, the theory starts from the idea that the 'natural lottery' produces differences in talents which from a moral point of view, are arbitrary. This forms a basis for claims to compensation: unchosen differences are unjust and must be collectively insured.[5]

Relational egalitarianism's central principle is equality of standing between citizens. Relational egalitarians reject self-ownership (in contrast to both forms of libertarianism). However, relational egalitarians also reject luck egalitarians' focus on compensating for bad brute luck (Anderson, 1999, 2010). Their basic intuition is that justice is not a matter of compensating for bad fortune, but of providing citizens with equality in some other dimension, i.e. the intersubjective dimension of their standing in society. In practical terms, this is translated into a distributive principle for external resources, which can be more or less egalitarian. Some defend a sufficientarian principle, which focuses on a threshold level of resources or capabilities for all citizens (Anderson, 1999; Nussbaum, 2000), while others focus on a principle maximising the position of the worse off (Rawls, 1999).

All three theories propose a more egalitarian distribution of external resources than right-libertarianism. This implies a less-than-fully capitalist scheme of property rights. However, these theories present very different groundings for this claim. Left-libertarians work from the intuition that *external* resources, being originally owned by no one, belong to everyone equally. Their claim is primarily about the resources 'out there' and their rightful distribution. Luck egalitarians work from the moral arbitrariness of *internal* endowments. Their claim is primarily about individual responsibility and its limits, conceptualised along the lines of the choice/chance distinction. Relational egalitarians focus on the necessity of redistribution in order to attain equality of standing between citizens. Their focus is on an *intersubjective* state of equality (akin to republicans: being able to 'look each other in the eye'), and the necessary distributive preconditions for that intersubjective state.

Let's now connect these normative theories to the question of property. Right-libertarianism provides a more-or-less direct link with a capitalist economy of maximally extensive property rights. The other theories exhibit an *increasing conceptual distance* from the concept of property. Left-libertarianism is, like right-libertarianism, conceptually organised around the concepts of self-ownership and world-ownership. Justice for both types of libertarians is about the distribution of property, albeit they each propose a different distribution. Luck-egalitarianism occupies a middle position. On the one hand, its argument about internal endowments is not couched directly in terms of property rights, since it doesn't claim that internal endowments are collective property (even if no one can help being born with more or less of them). Nonetheless, its treatment of internal endowments is akin to property, since differences in them do become the subject of claims of redistribution (via insurance). Although differences in endowments cannot be redistributed as property, monetary compensation for differences in endowments can. Finally, the relational egalitarian position does not conceive of justice as a claim to property. Its normative focus is on the structure of intersubjective relations. Of course claims to resources can be related to this normative claim by way of an empirical claim, but the link is more distant in conceptual terms.

The reason for these differences, I suspect, is that libertarian and egalitarian theories differ in one crucial respect: the former start from a puzzle about the ownership of resources, whereas the latter start from a normative conception of persons. This has profound consequences.

Libertarian theories, both in their right-wing and their left-wing forms, give pride of place to the problem of 'how to divide the pie'. They presuppose a picture in which persons with moral standing confront the fact that there are both internal and external assets whose rightful possession has to be assigned to individuals. The possible disputes about the ownership of these assets forces upon the agents the question 'who gets what?' Hence the question about property is central to these theories from the start. The central topic of a theory of justice simply is how to solve the problem of assigning property rights. The different conceptualisations of original property (self-owned, unowned, commonly owned) and just property assignments (where left- and right-libertarians split ways) should not detract from this underlying similarity. By contrast, egalitarian theories take off from a different description of the problem of justice, as about 'what persons owe to each other'. Being a member of the same group (political community) involves certain duties towards other persons in the group. Luck egalitarians argue that it is essential that no inequalities that were not under a person's control arise in a political community. Relational egalitarians argue that citizens in the same political community should stand in relations of equality with one another. In both cases an idea of the person's attributes compared to other person's attributes sets the theory in motion.

Of course, this does not mean that libertarian theories do not contain a conception of the person, or that egalitarian theories do not contain ideas about the distribution of property. To argue for conclusions about self-ownership and world-ownership, libertarians resort to some ideal of negative freedom. The person is seen as an independent individual who can claim non-interference from others. Property should be arranged so as to defend this claim. Reversely, egalitarians do argue about property. For example, Dworkin's conclusion about equality of external resources is an institutional translation of this moral view about the relevance of luck between persons. Nonetheless, the order is different. For libertarians the problem of property comes first, and the conception of the person is used in answering the question of property. For egalitarians the problem of justice is about persons, their attributes and mutual relations. The distribution of property serves to realise the desired ideal in terms of these attributes and relations.

Despite this split between egalitarian and libertarian theories, we should also keep in mind another split, between right-libertarianism and the other three theories. The latter all work – albeit in very different ways – with a dichotomy between 'individual' versus 'social' claims. All of them argue (on a different moral basis) that individuals have a claim on society to receive some resources, even though they haven't worked for them. This anti-capitalist social claim, however, *is not necessarily a claim of property*; it is an undifferentiated category, which may point to various institutional alternatives, with very different effects. It functions more like a metaphor, a stand-in for various alternative institutions, than a conclusion about the forms that anti-capitalist property would need to take (this is true for all three dimensions of property: who should be owning property, which rights should be given to property-owners, and which things should be allowed to be objects of property rights). Only left-libertarianism seems to interpret this social claim as a property claim (but see below in the last section).

With these differences in mind, let's now turn to solidarism, and see how it should be located amidst the theoretical landscape sketched so far. I will do so in two steps: first by comparing the similarities and differences between solidarism and left-libertarianism, then by analysing the alleged opposition between solidarism and egalitarianism.

Solidarism as a form of left-libertarianism?

In the typology of four theories used in this paper, solidarism is closest to left-libertarianism. In this section, I will attempt a systematic reconstruction of the similarities and differences between both types of theory.

In Kohn's reconstruction (on which I rely here), solidarism rests strongly on Alfred Fouillé's argument against Locke. Fouillé argued that Locke's argument for private property had to be modified. The fact that a person mixes his labour with an external resource implies only private ownership to the extent of the labour one has invested. External resources have value, and this value remains social. Hence we need to recognise both individual and social property in the product, which is a mixture of labour and nature. If the individual appropriates all, he dispossesses others of a part of nature that they can rightfully claim as theirs. This in turn becomes the basis for a claim to social rights funded by all (Kohn, 2016, pp. 607–610, this issue). This argument clearly follows the left-libertarian scheme of combining the self-ownership of my labour with the shared ownership of external resources. Kohn acknowledges the latter where she embraces an explanation of solidarism in terms of the world-ownership thesis (Kohn, this issue). However, as far as I can see there are three important departures from left-libertarianism.

First, as Kohn explains, the solidarists argued that 'the self' should also be seen as a social construction. Growing up to become a participant in society requires the caring work of others, thus one is born with a 'debt' to society. Also in many other ways, one's own productivity depends on the linkages one has with others (externalities). All of these factors also form a basis for accepting an obligation to pay off one's debts to society (Kohn, 2016, pp. 610–612). This is a very different line of argument, which is based on a luck-egalitarian intuition: that one cannot fully claim the fruits of one's own talents, since they were not under one's control.[6] This should be kept distinct from the idea that the common or equal ownership of external resources, even after labour has been used upon it, forms the proper basis for collective redistribution. Both lines of argument can of course be run in tandem (as luck egalitarians do when they also accept equality of external resources), but they are nonetheless distinct. (given the predominance of the social property thesis I will leave this part of solidarism out of consideration in what follows).

Second, Kohn provides a different *normative basis* for solidarism, namely in the fact of being member of a cooperative venture. It is the interdependence and proximity of citizens within a given society which gives each of them a claim upon others (Kohn, this issue). This stands in marked contrast to (at least some) left-libertarian theories which argue for an individual's right to a share of all external resources on the planet (Steiner, 2005). In the latter, being a human being rather than being a member of a society is the basis for the individual's claim.[7] However, this difference should not obscure the essential similarity between solidarism and left-libertarianism in its endorsement of the social property claim of individuals on all external goods (either within society or in the whole world). For both, this claim stands in contrast to liberal-egalitarian theories of justice. However, as I will argue in the final section, the membership claim does raise questions about the difference in the justification strategies used by solidarists and egalitarians.

Third, Kohn argues that – in contrast to left-libertarians – solidarists focus less on maximising individual freedom, and more on fostering a shared ethos in society. Concretely, this means they endorsed public schools, public places and other forms of 'collective consumption and experience' (Kohn, this issue). The dispute here is about the form public expenditures should take once the social property claim has led to taxation of those who owe a debt to society (the rich). One can either give everyone an individualised share of social property (the left-libertarian strategy) or provide collective, non-divisible goods (solidarism). However, it should immediately be noted that many social rights (such as a right to access to public services like education or health care) do take the form of individualised benefits. This, the solidarist cannot deny. On the other hand, liberal egalitarians can also argue for public goods provision as a necessary condition for the sustenance of a liberal society (Miller, 2004). Hence, while this feature differentiates solidarism from left-libertarianism, the difference with liberal egalitarians seems overblown.

In conclusion, solidarism does share a very important similarity with left-libertarianism, in its endorsement of a claim to social property. However, I have noted three important differences: in terms of the social origin of the self, the normative basis in social membership, and the preference for public goods provisioning as a means of developing a shared ethos. On each of these points, solidarism is less individualist, and indeed more 'social' (i.e. more concerned to theorise the embeddedness of an individual's existence in a social context, its prerequisites and its consequences) in its orientation than left-libertarianism. However, each of these points also brings solidarism closer to (at least some forms of) egalitarianism. Let's now bring out this comparison more systematically.

Solidarism versus liberal egalitarianism

Solidarism is seen by Kohn as distinctively superior to the dominant left-wing theory opposing right-libertarian capitalism, which she refers to as welfare-state capitalism, or, provocatively, the 'welfare-as-state-charity-model'.[8] She identifies welfare-state capitalism with the normative theory of liberal egalitarianism and criticises this theory on substantive grounds. In this section, I will analyse this debate between egalitarians and solidarists on the most convincing basis for arguing for a welfare state.

In her first article, Kohn argues that the solidaristic theory, with its emphasis on social property and social debt, provides an alternative justification to this model, since it shows why taxation so as to provide social rights is not a matter of forcing charity upon the rich (those who pay the taxes), but reparation for what the rich have taken from the rest by their disproportionate appropriation of resources within the capitalist production process (Kohn, 2016, pp. 604, 622). Here the emphasis is very strongly on framing advantages of property claims: while charity is based upon moral claims to help those in need which are largely left to individuals' own assessment of what they owe to others, property claims are the basis of politically enforced redistribution. However, while I agree that framing the welfare state as a form of state charity renders the basis of welfare services rather weak, I do not see how one can claim that historically the left has argued for the welfare state on the basis of the idea of charity. Defending the welfare state was about making a claim about social rights from the start, as

Kohn implicitly agrees when briefly mentioning T.H. Marshall's famous defence of social rights (Kohn, 2016, p. 604). Her criticism of Marshall is that he didn't provide a normative foundation of such claims. In her second article, the argument takes a different turn. Here, she seems to grant that liberal egalitarian theories can argue for social rights to welfare (i.e. not mere charity), and discusses several egalitarians who have done so. Here, her argument is that the basis of these egalitarian claims lies in an ideal of individual autonomy (she focuses on the theories of Fabre [1998] and Gewirth [1996]), to which she objects on substantive grounds.

Kohn's argument is that given the assumption of individual autonomy, liberal egalitarianism makes individuals themselves responsible for providing for their own welfare. This leads to three problems. First, it is unclear how others – and in particular the state – can come in as duty bearers. After all, there are also other things individuals may need (such as love) which no one has a duty to provide. Second, to mark off how much others are obliged to help, we need to find out at which at which points individuals cannot any longer be held responsible for lacks in their welfare. This is highly indeterminate: how to make the distinction between the deserving and the undeserving poor? Overcoming this problem in order to be able to make decisions about social benefits requires a highly intrusive and paternalist state. Third, even if this would be successful in practice, Kohn still seems to have a problem with the conditional, residual scheme of rights this offers. Solidarism endorses a welfare state that not only avoids being intrusive and paternalist, but also offers much stronger, unconditional rights to everyone (Kohn, this issue). In sum, liberal egalitarians have problems with duty-bearers, threshold setting, and conditionality.

In my response, I will grant that liberal egalitarianism is best reconstructed – along the lines of Fabre and Gewirth – as relying on a substantive concept of autonomy (for my elaboration of such a view, and its extension to the question of property, see Claassen, 2015, in press). Others may want to criticise Kohn for not realising that some forms of liberal egalitarianism do not rely on strong metaphysical commitments to autonomy (Rawls's political liberalism being the primary example), but can defend the welfare state on a thinner, allegedly politically neutral basis. Since I do not find these claims attractive, I will leave such criticisms to others.

Let's first address the issue of conditionality. The solidarist argument here runs the risk of attacking a straw man. It is unclear that liberal egalitarian theories that start from the idea that individuals have a right to the (material and other) preconditions for becoming individually autonomous beings, cannot accommodate the idea of unconditional public services. The template of cash benefits may here be misleading. Services in kind, such as public education and public health care, can very well be seen as services that must be provided unconditionally and equally to all citizens to help them be autonomous beings. Similarly, liberal egalitarianism could also defend an unconditional basic income as necessary for individual independence and autonomy. This only points to the identification of theoretical space within liberal egalitarianism to accommodate Kohn's criticism more than she thinks it can. Another line of response would be to counter by asking whether conditionality is always wrong. This admittedly is a large debate, but I am not yet convinced that it always is a disadvantage when a theory makes some forms of welfare provisioning conditional on inability to work or other conditions.

Second, there is the issue of threshold setting. Conditionality requires distinguishing the deserving from the undeserving poor and this can only be done by turning the state into a punitive state. In response, one should note that egalitarians are split on this issue. Kohn rightly targets luck egalitarians for needing this distinction, but she doesn't note the influential counterattack by relational egalitarians, who have criticised luck egalitarianism on exactly this point (Anderson, 1999). I would like to go one step further, however, and note that relational egalitarians also rely on a threshold, marking who does and who does not get a claim to social rights, albeit a different one. For them the threshold is not set at the point where 'responsibility' or 'control' over one's actions starts or ends; but at some sufficiency threshold, however, defined (I restrict myself to sufficientarian versions of relational egalitarianism, see above). This suggests it is not so easy to escape defining some threshold to operationalise citizens' claim to a given set of social rights. Without such a threshold state provision would be limitless. Arguably, solidarism doesn't want to defend limitless claims, so it would also need a way to define a cut-off point, and would then be in the same boat as egalitarianism.

Third, the question of rights and duties. Why do some, but not other interests – with interests defined as things we need to reach an autonomous life – become the subject of rights, and hence the basis of a claim that others have a duty? Kohn claims the liberal tradition gives a tautological answer on this point. I think this question cannot be answered in general, since different theorists reconstruct the process of the generation of rights and duties differently. To confine myself to one of Kohn's targets, Gewirth, he gives a perfectly sensible account of how it is implicit in every person's stance as an agent, to claim that others ought not to interfere with one's conditions of agency, and in some cases, to help provide the conditions for agency. Duties are the basis, and rights are claimed as correlative to duties. In a second step, some but not all of these moral duties are then attributed to the state as institutional representative of the moral community as a whole (Gewirth, 1978). His argument for doing so is long and complicated, but more engagement with it – and with the arguments from other liberal authors – is necessary to establish that the liberal tradition is tautological in its defence of autonomy rights.

I hope these replies establish that egalitarianism does have the resources to counter Kohn's criticisms, and shows that both may be more closely connected than is sometimes realised. Finally, I want to address an important point about Kohn's membership justification for solidarism.

My worry is that the membership justification underlying the social property claim is either implausible or indistinguishable from liberal egalitarianism. Remember that the idea is to see society as a cooperative venture. This may be interpreted by solidarists as giving members a share of social wealth as a compensation for their contribution to society, due to them because their original, market-based compensation (e.g. wages) does not reflect the share of social wealth that they are owed. Kohn is very clear about rejecting this compensatory interpretation (Kohn, this issue). This seems sensible, but it does mean that one's membership in the cooperative venture must be understood very minimally, as one's mere presence in society (even if one does not contribute productively). But thus understood, one may wonder what the difference is with arguing that one deserves a share of social wealth simply because one is an individual with the capacities for autonomy? There is at least one normative theory that exactly makes this move. C.B. MacPherson famously argued for property in the means of production for all (Macpherson, 1973, pp. 120–140, 1985, pp. 76–85) and based this on a concept of positive freedom, of realising 'men's human powers, that is, their potential for using and developing their uniquely human capacities' (Macpherson, 1973, p. 4). For him this was both a property right and a human right, he deliberately fused both categories. This example shows how liberal-egalitarian theories may come to conclusions with respect to the distribution of social wealth similar to those of solidarists.

In conclusion, solidarism and other left-libertarian theories seem to share the same structural potential and problems as egalitarians, when arguing in favour of a more egalitarian society than right-libertarians argue for, characterised by the provisioning of social rights. In contrast to right-libertarians, all of them make what I have called a 'social claim' (see Section 2), which can be, but doesn't necessarily have to be, cashed out in terms of a concept of social property. If my last argument is correct, than the solidarist (and arguably also the left-libertarian) view that this is a property claim is not the final word, since this claim in the end goes back to a deeper principle to determine who has a property claim (such as autonomy or membership in a community). The solidarists' point that the value of the wealth we hold is socially determined to a much larger extent than we may be conscious of is a powerful one. But so is the point that the conditions for becoming an autonomously functioning individual are much more socially determined than we may normally realise. The idea of an isolated individual is a chimera on both counts and the potential force in terms of political rhetoric should be equally powerful. These ideas could – and I think should – be defended in tandem.

Notes

1. More precisely, Gaus defines capitalism as the conjunction of three institutional elements: maximally extensive property rights, efficient markets and firms led

in the interests of their owners. But the latter two elements he derives from the idea of maximally extensive property.

2. As an alternative, first-occupation instead of labour-mixing may be the justificatory ground. (Narveson, 2001, p. 79). Conceptually, these appear close cousins, since 'grabbing' an object may be treated as mixing one's labour with it in a rather minimal sense.

3. I am not arguing this case is convincing, even on its own terms. Most importantly, a defence of capitalism doesn't follow as straightforwardly as presented here in the main text to the extent that (1) the libertarian theory includes a Lockean proviso, and/or (2) the principle of rectification is applied to rectify wrongful transfers. Many libertarians downplay these potential problems.

4. There has been debate about the coherence of the acceptance of self-ownership and the defence of an egalitarian distribution of world-ownership (Fried, 2004). However, let's assume a coherent position is possible.

5. Luck egalitarians differ on whether all differences in talents are unchosen, hence whether all economic differences arising from the exertion of talents should be equalised (Cohen, 1989, p. 922). Here for simplicity's sake I assume they are.

6. Kohn argues that one of the solidarists (Leon Bourgeois) used an explicitly luck egalitarian argument about choice and chance (Kohn, 2016, p. 616). This raises the question why in the second article Kohn distances herself from luck egalitarianism (Kohn, this issue). Whatever of that, I would argue that luck egalitarianism is implicit in the solidarists' endorsement of the socialisation (not just of external resources, but also) of the fruits of individual productive labour.

7. Kohn's argument here shares a lot with recent arguments to justify human rights to membership in society (Cohen, 2004). If membership is indeed central for Kohn, then it is not the claim to a share of the society's collective property itself which grounds a set of human rights (in particular here: social rights), as in Matthias Risse's theory of human rights (Risse, 2009, 2012). Rather, membership in a society comes first in terms of normative justification, and collective property, generated as a spin-off of social activity in that society, is a way of expressing the claims of membership.

8. Historically, solidarism was contrasted on the left-wing of the spectrum with socialism (Kohn, 2016, p. 604), but here I will follow Kohn in leaving this out of consideration and focusing on welfare state capitalism as the contemporary opponent of solidarism.

Acknowledgements

I would like to thank audiences at the Workshop on 'Approaches to Public Goods: Solidarity and Social Justice' (Toronto, May 2016), at the Economic Ethics Network Meeting (Barcelona, July 2016) and at the Annual Conference of the World Interdisciplinary Network for Institutional Research (Boston, September 2016). In particular I would like to thank Margaret Kohn, Igor Shoikhedbrod and Avigail Ferdman, as well as two anonymous reviewers of this journal, for their comments. The Netherlands Organisation for Scientific Research contributed funding under project no. 360-20-390.

Disclosure statement

No potential conflict of interest was reported by the author.

References

Anderson, E. (1999). What is the point of equality? *Ethics, 109*, 287–337.

Anderson, E. (2010). The fundamental disagreement between luck egalitarians and relational egalitarians. *Canadian Journal of Philosophy, Supplementary, 36*, 1–24.

Becker, L. (1977). *Property rights. Philosophic foundations*. London: Routledge & Kegan Paul.

Christman, J. (1994). *The myth of property. Toward an egalitarian theory of ownership*. New York: Oxford University Press.

Claassen, R. (2015). The capability to hold property. *Journal of Human Development and Capabilities, 16*, 220–236.

Claassen, R. (in press). An agency-based capability theory of justice. *European Journal of Philosophy*.

Cohen, G. A. (1989). On the currency of egalitarian justice. *Ethics, 99*, 906–944.

Cohen, J. (2004). Minimalism about human rights: The most we can hope for? *Journal of Political Philosophy, 12*, 190–213.

Dagan, H., & Heller, M. (2001). The liberal commons. *The Yale Law Journal, 110*, 549–623.

Dworkin, R. (2000). *Sovereign virtue. The theory and practice of equality*. Cambridge, MA: Harvard University Press.

Fabre, C. (1998). Constitutionalising social rights. *Journal of Political Philosophy, 6*, 263–284.

Fried, B. (2004). Left-libertarianism: A review essay. *Philosophy & Public Affairs, 32*, 66–92.

Gaus, G. (2010). The idea and ideal of capitalism. In G. Brenkert & T. Beauchamp (Eds.), *The Oxford handbook of business ethics* (pp. 73–99). Oxford: Oxford University Press.

Gewirth, A. (1978). *Reason and morality*. Chicago, IL: The University of Chicago Press.

Gewirth, A. (1996). *The community of rights*. Chicago, IL: The University of Chicago Press.

Honoré, A. M. (1987). Ownership. In *Making law bind. Essays legal and philosophical* (pp. 161–192). Oxford: Clarendon Press.

Kohn, M. (2016). The critique of possessive individualism: Solidarism and the city. *Political Theory, 44*, 603–628.

Kohn, M. (This issue). Solidarism and social rights. *Critical Review of International Social and Political Philosophy*.

Lehavi, A. (2008). Mixing property. *Seton Hall Law Review, 38*, 137–212.

Locke, J. (2003). *Two treatises of government*. New Haven, CT: Yale University Press.

Mack, E. (2002). Self-ownership, Marxism and egalitarianism, part II: Challenges to the self-ownership thesis. *Politics, Philosophy & Economics, 1*, 237–276.

Macpherson, C. B. (1973). *Democratic theory: Essays in retrieval*. Oxford: Clarendon Press.

Macpherson, C. B. (1985). *The rise and fall of economic justice and other papers*. Oxford: Oxford University Press.

Miller, D. (2004). Justice, democracy and public goods. In K. Dowding, R. Goodin, & C. Pateman (Eds.), *Justice and democracy. Essays for Brian Barry* (pp. 127–149). Cambridge: Cambridge University Press.

Munzer, S. (1990). *A theory of property*. Cambridge: Cambridge University Press.

Narveson, J. (2001). *The libertarian idea*. Ontario: Broadview Press.

Nozick, R. (1974). *Anarchy, state, and utopia*. Oxford: Blackwell.

Nussbaum, M. (2000). *Women and human development. The capabilities approach*. Cambridge: Cambridge University Press.

Otsuka, M. (1998). Self-ownership and equality: A lockean reconciliation. *Philosophy & Public Affairs, 27*, 65–92.

Rawls, J. (1999). *A theory of justice*. revised. Oxford: Oxford University Press.

Risse, M. (2009). Common ownership of the earth as a non-parochial standpoint: A contingent derivation of human rights. *European Journal of Philosophy, 17*, 277–304.

Risse, M. (2012). *On global justice*. Princeton, NJ: Princeton University Press.

Ryan, A. (1984). *Property and political theory*. New York, NY: Basil Blackwell.

Steiner, H. (1994). *An essay on rights*. Oxford: Blackwell.

Steiner, H. (2005). Territorial justice and global redistribution. In G. Brock & H. Brighouse (Eds.), *The political philosophy of cosmopolitanism* (pp. 28–38). Cambridge: Cambridge University Press.

van Parijs, P. (1995). *Real freedom for all. What (if anything) can justify capitalism?* Oxford: Oxford University Press.

Waldron, J. (1988). *The right to private property*. Oxford: Clarendon Press.

Engaging the reluctant taxpayer

Michael Joel Kessler

ABSTRACT

A commitment to political neutrality means that citizens have a legitimate complaint when the coercive power of the state is used to advance some particular conception of how it is good to live. In this paper I investigate how to address this complaint in the case of public funding for the arts. There are two promising ways to justify public arts spending. First, as Thomas Nagel argues, the arts are a source of intrinsic values and so command our respect. I reject this argument because intrinsic values are not automatically political values. Second, Ronald Dworkin argues that access to the arts is required to fully participate in social life. This argument draws a connection between the arts and citizenship and so fares better in establishing a political justification for the arts. However, Dworkin relies on the special value of high art relative to popular art, which undermines the neutrality of his argument. I show that a justification can be given that does not depend on the high value of the arts. I develop an account that shows how the arts can support just relations between citizens. This account is in keeping with a liberal commitment to neutrality.

The taxpayer's challenge

When citizens reasonably disagree about the good what duties does this impose on governments? One answer is that states must remain neutral. This means citizens have a legitimate complaint when the coercive power of the state is used to advance some particular conception of how it is good to live. Supposing this is a foundational commitment of one's theory of justice, the question remains of how this applies at various levels of government. In this paper I want to focus on how neutrality regulates the projects and goals that are funded through taxation, specifically public funding for the arts.

There are three possible lines one could take here: (1) argue that the demand of neutrality *does not* apply to public funding in general and show that public support for the arts is a legitimate state end, (2) argue that the demand of neutrality *does* apply to public funding and show that arts funding *cannot* be justified, and (3) argue that the demand of neutrality *does* apply to public funding and funding the arts *can* be justified.

I defend this last position. I argue that the arts provide distinctive means for pursuing legitimate state ends. I am going to proceed by trying to address the concerns of an imagined character called *the reluctant sufficientarian taxpayer*.[1] For the sufficientarian taxpayer, the fundamental justification for political authority is to establish the independence of each individual. Like his libertarian counterpart, he thinks that the protection of individual rights is the central function of political authority. The sufficientarian, non-libertarian, aspect of this view is that each is entitled to call on the state to help when one's position as independent is threatened. State institutions therefore must play both a protecting and supporting role to realize the independence of each person over the course of a life.[2]

On this view, to be an independent agent means reaching and staying above a threshold. The content of the threshold is complex, but generally refers to a person's ability to form, pursue, and revise ends of her own. The reason this view is sufficientarian and not strictly egalitarian is that some people will be much more free than others to revise and pursue their ends due to resources like wealth and talent. What matters for the sufficientarian taxpayer is that everyone be (and remain) above the threshold, not that everyone be above it to the same extent.

Taxation is justifiable, on this view, only if it advances some purpose related to protecting the independence of each person. Spending tax dollars on the arts lacks a straightforward connection to this goal and is therefore *prima facie* wrong.

There are many ways to respond to this argument. One way is to deny that the taxpayer has any special standing to demand justification for how tax dollars are spent. They are not 'his' dollars. This reply does not really meet the objection on its own terms. The role of taxpayer is just a different way of describing the role of citizen. And as citizens, we do have a special standing to demand justification for how our political institutions act. These are 'our' institutions and should not be used for private purposes.

One way to respond to the reluctant taxpayer on his own terms is to argue against the claim that the state would violate neutrality in supporting the arts. Thomas Nagel defends this view by arguing that the arts are a source of intrinsic values. Insofar as we all ought to recognize intrinsic values, public funding for the arts is justified. In Section II I will argue that Nagel does not succeed in showing that intrinsic values are political values. So his argument fails to answer the objection. In Section III I turn to Ronald Dworkin's attempt to justify spending on the arts as a means to ensuring access to our shared culture. I will show that despite his attempts to refrain from appealing to the superior value of the 'high' arts, he slips into some of the same assumptions about value that make Nagel's argument problematic.

In the final section, I propose an account of funding for the arts that meets the taxpayer's objections. My argument connects the arts to independence through the idea of citizenship. I propose three different political values – toleration, rectification, and identification – for which the arts can be a means. Each of these values falls under the general political idea of solidarity and my argument is that the arts can be a resource to strengthen solidarity between citizens.

Intrinsic value and public funding

Nagel (1991, p. 134) argues that intrinsic values can be pursued through political institutions:

> That there are things which are good in themselves, however, seems to me a position on which reasonable persons can be expected to agree, even if they do not agree about what those things are. And *acceptance of that position is enough to justify ordinary tax support* for a society's effort to identify and promote such goods, if it can effectively do so – provided it does not engage in repression or intolerance of those who would have chosen different candidates.

Nagel's argument is fairly straightforward: reasonable people will agree that there are intrinsically good objects, and *if* those objects can be realized through public financing then each reasonable person should be willing to devote taxes to that end.

There are two ways to read Nagel's argument. Naively understood his point is that since experts agree that some works of art are intrinsically valuable, we should fund the creation of art including paying the experts to tell us what to fund. Nagel encourages this interpretation in arguing that 'there has to be a general willingness to accept the judgment of experts in deciding what to support' even by those who are not 'personally interested in fine art.' (p. 135) The naïve reading, however, omits the heart of Nagel's argument: intrinsic goods are things for which *respect* is 'the appropriate attitude.' The fact that respect is owed to such objects explains why funding them through public funds is legitimate.

The first step of this argument is conceptual. To acknowledge something as 'good in itself' is to recognize that it has a value that does not reduce to our enjoyment of it. Rather, we enjoy it *because* it is good. This makes such goods different in kind from ordinary goods. The second step of Nagel's argument is to show that intrinsic goods 'have an important role in political justification' (p. 132). Nagel claims: 'such values provide legitimate goals for a society. By calling these goals legitimate I mean that reasonable persons *ought* to agree that resources […] should be used to further such ends' (p. 133, my emphasis).

The reason he thinks we are under rational pressure to support public funding is that 'everyone has reason to want the state to identify and encourage excellence' (p. 134). If true, this step secures his conclusion: insofar as we are

SOLIDARITY AND PUBLIC GOODS

rational we see that intrinsic values ought to be realized. We recognize that public institutions, through their formidable resources, are in a position to bring about some of 'the best things in the world.' We all have reason to support activities that embody artistic excellence. This justifies devoting public funds to creating and staffing institutions like museums, galleries, and the National Endowment for Arts.

Nagel agrees that neutrality regulates the state's involvement in reasonable disagreements. However, since the realization of intrinsic goods cannot reasonably be rejected, there are no objections based in neutrality to public funding for the arts. Thus, Nagel's response to the reluctant taxpayer is that public support for the arts is justified because it realizes values that *should* belong to each of us, insofar as we are rational. The taxpayer's reluctance is not a valid objection because he is wrong about the worth of the values in question.

There is an obvious perfectionist slant to this argument. As Nagel puts the point, 'beauty and understanding are valuable even if they are appreciated only by a minority, and a society that does not recognize this is *impoverished*' (p. 132, my emphasis). Nagel addresses worries about the scope of perfectionism by noting that his argument does not provide an unlimited license to be used, for example, to promote a specific religion. When reasonable people can disagree then the usual requirement of neutrality applies. Mandatory public support is limited to cases where the value is intrinsic.

Leaving aside whether Nagel's argument successfully constrains his perfectionism to the domain of artistic expression, we can question whether the principles he employs are sound. Nagel's central premise is that when abiding by the correct rational norms we would recognize that excellent artistic works deserve our respect and financial support. This is the key premise in securing his conclusion: 'the promotion of what is excellent is, under that description, a valid collective goal even for an involuntary association like the state' (p. 134). Without this premise, mandatory support for the arts would unjustifiably be forcing people to support some particular conception of the good.

While Nagel never says so explicitly, his argument relies on the undefended assumption that failure to give support to the realization of intrinsically valuable objects makes one *unreasonable*. We can see this assumption at work in two places. First, his argument is addressed to people who grant that some goods are intrinsically valuable but disagree about *which* objects instantiate that good. His conclusion is that all such people should accept public arts funding even when they disagree with what ends up being funded. Nagel does not address his argument to those who disagree that there are intrinsically valuable objects. This is odd since these people will also be forced to pay into the tax pool that funds the arts.

This omission is not by itself a refutation of Nagel's argument since he captures those people in a different part of the argument. He argues that since intrinsically valuable objects make a claim on all of us, it is permissible to use the coercive institution of taxation to achieve this end. 'By calling these goals legitimate I mean that reasonable people *ought* to agree that the resources of the state [...] should be used to further such ends' (p. 133, my emphasis). This premise needs to be defended, *not* to people who deny the possibility of intrinsic value, but rather to those who deny that the creation of intrinsic value is a justification for coercive taxation. This step is critical in successfully justifying mandatory public funding of the arts within an involuntary association like the state.

The reluctant taxpayer will not be convinced by this argument. His objection is that intrinsic values are not, for that reason, political values. Nagel may well be right that the tax-payer is failing to recognize reasons that apply to him. His reluctance would then be unreasonable in some sense. However, Nagel still needs to show that we are entitled to ignore his complaints. All the taxpayer is saying is 'don't enlist me in this project unless you can make the case that I am undermining someone's independence by withholding my support.' Nagel attempts to circumvent this objection by claiming that no reasonable person could disclaim the responsibility to help bring about what is truly beautiful. But even if this is true, this does not show that others would be licensed to use the coercive institution of taxation to force compliance.

In short, Nagel argues that when people are being unreasonable we can force them to do what they have reason to do. There is, however, a gap between showing that everyone ought to do X, and the claim that everyone can be forced to do X.[3] There are many things that people have reason to pursue, like meaningful relationships or their own moral perfection, but the intrinsic value contained in these activities is insufficient – by itself – to justify additional mandatory taxation. As such, Nagel's claim that 'society should try to foster the creation and preservation of what is best' (p. 135) is problematic if what he means is that everyone can be forced to contribute to this end.

In this argument, we can see that Nagel does not track the justificatory difference between saying that there is reason for *each of us* to do something and saying that there is a reason for *us* to do something. Public reasons are not public because they are universal. Rather, they are public because their content is derived from ends we share *as citizens*.

In sum, we can agree with Nagel that some objects are 'among the best things in the world' but deny his conclusion that no one has a valid complaint against being taxed to realize these objects.

Art, choice, and culture

Dworkin (1985) defends the thesis that funding the arts is required to protect society against decay. This argument doesn't depend directly on the intrinsic value of art, but on the connection between the arts and the underlying structure of society. His conclusion is that 'art makes a general contribution to the community as a whole, not just to those who enter into special commercial transactions to enjoy it' (p. 225).

Dworkin's argument rests on two ideas: (1) all aspects of culture are inextricably intertwined, and (2) a culture should protect against the loss of its valuable aspects. The first claim is uncontroversial. While we can draw a distinction between popular and high culture, these cannot be divorced entirely. All aspects of culture form a 'seamless web' and they 'influence one another reciprocally' (p. 225). Nevertheless, there are distinct formal structures in high culture. The way opera combines music and theater is unique to that art form, and cannot be replicated by going to a play on Friday and then to a concert on Saturday. Supposing that there is something distinctive about the form of high art, Dworkin next considers the way that high culture affects the underlying structure of society. High art provides a reference for more popular works of art and leads to a valuable cultural 'spillover'. For example, movies will replicate the structure of Greek comedies and tragedies. In this way, high culture provides general culture with *resonance*. '[These] specific references [...] supply not just a convenient set of ideas easily invoked, but a set of ideas valuable exactly because they are identified as belonging to high culture and therefore as having a distinct aesthetic value' (p. 225).

We now move to the second phase of the argument. If we don't institute measures to make sure that popular culture is in contact with high art, then the beneficial effects of resonance won't occur. Spillover requires access, and if high art moves exclusively into the hands of the very wealthy, this will worsen the culture as a whole by removing the possibility of cultural resonance. To this point, Dworkin has not said anything that would justify public expenditure to the reluctant taxpayer. 'So what,' he might ask, 'why does the fact that some aspect of our culture would become a luxury just for the rich make a claim on the rest of us?'

Dworkin's reply involves thinking about the context in which individuals make choices. He argues that culture provides the structure within which we act, and that access to the arts is a condition on making valuable choices within that structure. Dworkin defends this point through an analogy with language. Language has two noteworthy structural features. First, it is intrinsically social. Language allows a speaker to connect with her audience. Connecting with an audience is not just a means to being heard but also a means to being *understood*. Second, language can be more or less sophisticated and this affects the meaning that can be expressed. Nuances of vocabulary and style within a language allow for more precise and profound statements. For example, irony can often be a more compelling way of making a point than direct assertion. If language is valuable as a means to being understood, then precision matters as well. Properly conveying one's thoughts, feelings, or goals to others depends on all parties having access to the right words and concepts, but also shared modes and styles of expression.

Like language, art is a form of address that depends on the presence of an audience. The audience must be fluent in the distinctive modes of artistic expression if the address is to be understood. This confirms Dworkin's point that high and low art share a background structure, and it is that structure that makes it possible to appreciate the meaning of artistic expression. In order to recognize something as a work of art, we have to be able to fit it into a framework. Even counter-cultural artistic works (such as atonal musical compositions or art displays consisting of garbage scraps) need us to recognize them as fighting against certain conventions.[4]

Dworkin's point that artistic expression presupposes a shared structure is hard to dispute, however this will not move the reluctant taxpayer very much. While access to the structure enables one to engage in certain forms of expression, this does not show that anyone is *entitled* to this access. There is a clear enough sense in which we need a language to be independent. We need to be able to engage in transactions, to defend ourselves in court, to call the police and so on. But access to the arts is not a precondition to any of these things, so it is not clear what work Dworkin's analogy is supposed to do. If we are not able to communicate in the language of the arts then what follows? Whatever loss of freedom this involves does not obviously undermine our independence as citizens.

For Dworkin, the importance of access to high art can be demonstrated by considering the social loss we would suffer in its absence. Our culture contains aspects that are attributable to high art. This makes the culture better than it would be without high art. Dworkin is careful to note that the sense of 'better' he intends is that high culture expands the range of expressive options available, and not that it keeps the more valuable options open. If his argument were to rely on the superiority of high art, then it would violate the requirement of neutrality. To illustrate his point that artistic expression make society *impartially* better, Dworkin asks us to imagine a society in which no one has discovered narrative invention or storytelling. There is nothing perfectionist in asserting that such a society would be poorer than our own. It would be poorer because people would lack a means of expression beyond the literal. One need not adopt any particular conception of the good to recognize this as an impoverishment.

Dworkin thinks the same general point can be made for the distinctive expressive value of the 'high' arts. As such, we should make sure they remain alive and accessible in our culture. By funding the arts, we should think of ourselves as 'trustees for protecting the richness of our culture for those who will live their lives in it after us' (p. 229).

We come then to Dworkin's conclusion that public funding for the arts is a legitimate public end. High art has a distinctive value that is enmeshed in the cultural fabric of society. The reluctant taxpayer cannot coherently claim that he has not benefited from the richness of his culture. Therefore, he has an obligation to leave his culture at least as rich for others as he found it. This means funding access to high art so that the benefit of cultural resonance between high and low art will persist into the future.

The argument that the arts add to the range of expression is powerful. However, as I will show Dworkin does not succeed in avoiding reliance on non-public values. Recall the argument is supposed to work without depending on bettering the *content* of the individual's choice. Rather the benefit in question is *formal*: the freedom of choice of all members of society is improved when the distinctive form of high art is accessible. By appealing to a formal rather than a substantive idea of richness, Dworkin intends to avoid the non-neutral perfectionism of Nagel's argument.

The issue at hand is whether Dworkin is entitled to the premise that no one could reasonably disagree that 'it is *better* for people to have complexity and depth in the forms of life open to them' (p. 229, my emphasis). This is the core of the argument from cultural enrichment: any reasonable person would want a culturally vibrant society, so we have an obligation to leave society at least as rich as we found it and this requires continued public funding. There are two ideas at work in this argument and Dworkin does not sufficiently distinguish between them. The first idea is the formal claim that no one can object to having a richer set of opportunities because merely providing more options does not prevent anyone from choosing as she sees fit. This point is correct. However, this formal idea is not the main support for Dworkin's conclusion that the arts deserve to be supported through taxes. The hard work in his argument is done by the idea that it is *better* for society to contain 'complex and deep' options. This, I argue, invokes a substantive and not a formal notion of value.

The slip into a substantive conception of value can be seen at an earlier stage. When drawing the analogy between art and language Dworkin notes that there is nothing objectionable about protecting language from '*structural debasement or decay*' (p. 230, my emphasis). Just as losing a mode of expression can structurally impoverish a language; the same is true for artistic culture. However, as applied to art this would yield a far more radical conclusion than he wants. If his argument were formal in this way then *any* art making use of a distinctive form that risked extinction would be eligible for public support. The argument would be implausible if it implied that cultural richness depends on the preservation of *all* distinctive art forms.

One line of response open to Dworkin is to argue that it is only those artistic practices that demonstrate measurable 'cultural resonance' that should be preserved. Some art may indeed make use of a distinctive form, but this is not a sufficient condition for public support. Only the art whose absence from the general culture would lead to 'debasement' needs to be funded. This response would block the implication that all art forms should be publicly supported regardless of their social value.

However the argument is now open to the objection that it relies on a non-neutral conception of what is and is not worth protecting. How do we identify the artistic forms that lead to cultural resonance? Dworkin is clear that he wants to protect public access to things like the symphony, the opera, and impressionist painting. However, we can ask what would be lost if these become another thing the rich enjoy because they are rich.

Dworkin's answer is that these high art forms involve complexity and depth that is missing from popular art forms. Notice though that there is no risk that the kinds of artistic *practices* that Dworkin associates with high culture will disappear from the public sphere. Painting and sculpture and musical composition are part of popular culture as well as high culture. As such, the distinctive 'form' of high art is not at risk of receding from general society. Rather what seems more likely is that the privatization of art will mean that specific excellent *works* will disappear from publicly subsidized museums. And only the rich would be able to see Carmen performed by the best singers.

But now the structural aspect of the argument is doing no work: the value in question is the excellence manifested by these particular works. Once the 'decay and debasement' centers on what would happen if people were not given the opportunity to see a Monet with their own eyes, then this argument straightforwardly involves non-public values. Dworkin is trying to protect the very best works of art from disappearing into private collections. If this was to happen to all such works, it would certainly impoverish the rest of society. But it is implausible to suppose, this will lead to *structural* decay. One doesn't need to see a Monet in person to appreciate the distinctive value of impressionism. The structure is still there to be appreciated in the library book about Monet.

I have identified Dworkin's claim that 'it is better for people to have complexity and depth in the forms of life open to them' (p. 229) as the source of the dilemma in his argument. This claim can be interpreted in a formal way but then it is implausibly inclusive in its implications. When interpreted substantively, the claim embodies the non-neutral judgment that we should protect public access to what is most excellent because it is excellent.

One way to escape the dilemma on Dworkin's behalf is to show that the kind of complexity and depth he is talking about really is unique to high art but is still formal. This would block the implication that all distinctive art forms need to be preserved for all time while still being a neutral argument. On this interpretation each of us has a reason to want to be able to experience artistic practices that are complex and deep in addition to ones that are more simple. The reason is that as rational agents we can change our minds. If we are going to be able to make educated decisions about how the arts fit within our own lives, then we need to have experience with the complexity and depth that is exclusively present in high art. This version of Dworkin's argument rightly keeps the focus on enhancing the 'context of choice' (Kymlicka, 2004, p. 116) rather than on the excellence of high art.

Supposing this interpretation is plausible, does it provide a neutral and formal argument for subsidizing access to the best works of art, not because they are excellent but because they are complex and deep? One issue here is that this assumes that high art necessarily contains complexity and depth while low art necessarily lacks these. I won't press this issue because even this revised interpretation won't save Dworkin's overall argument.

On the revised view, we run into the same problem as before: the complexity and depth that (arguably) defines high art is already generally available in the culture. High art can be seen in books, studied in schools, and viewed in public galleries. I agree with Dworkin (and this revised version of his view) that public expenditure is needed to make sure the arts remain part of the educational system. However, a further argument is needed to show why this is not sufficient for one to receive the freedom-enhancing benefits that come from exposure to complexity. Absent this argument, there is no formal reason to object to the best works of art disappearing into private collections.

To sum up my objection, Dworkin's argument is supposed to avoid defending public support for what is excellent *because it is excellent*. I have argued it does not succeed in doing so. According to Dworkin's argument, the way to protect against this decay is to ensure that high art is in a position to have cultural resonance with lower art. I agree, but there is no reason to think this cultural resonance is at risk if only the rich can see the best artistic works and performances. A poor man's opera has the same structure as a rich man's opera, though obviously not its excellence. A revised Dworkinian argument that links access to excellence to enhancing the context of choice provides a more neutral justification. However, this will still fall short of justifying the kind of personal access to excellent works that Dworkin wants.

Art and citizenship

The requirement of neutrality means refraining from giving political preference to any one view of what makes a life meaningful. But this also means providing individuals with the opportunity to engage with diverse conceptions of the good, so that they can make choices that reflect authentic personal judgments. According to the theory of justice endorsed by the reluctant taxpayer, a just state must provide public education because in order to be independent all individuals must be in a position to make their own choices. Education makes us aware of the range of options that exist and provide us with the intellectual tools for adjudicating between them. When only the rich are educated, the independence of poor individuals is compromised. This is why access to education is required within a just society.

Using this argument, we can agree with Dworkin that the arts embody a distinctive mode of personal expression. We can agree with the revised Dworkinian argument that people need education in order to be in a position to appreciate the various forms that artistic expression can take. It follows that subsidies for access to the distinctive forms of 'high art' are legitimate. This justifies making the high arts part of general public education. There will of course be practical limits on what we can accommodate within a normal curriculum. States will need to strike a balance between cost and number of options. Given that we can't teach everything, we should be willing to defer to the judgments of experts regarding what ought to be taught in order to cover an appropriate range of aesthetic values. There will be winners and losers here just as there in most aspects of democratic life. So long as whatever is declared to be the teachable range of values is open to periodic review, this kind of public support for non-public values is unobjectionable.

This shows that non-public values, even very expensive ones, can be supported through mandatory taxation in the context of a valid public goal. This will justify art instruction in schools, books on high art for the library, and the occasional subsidized trip to very expensive galleries run for and by rich people. Is there any way to justify arts funding beyond the domain of public education? In what follows, I argue that citizenship can be a further basis for funding the arts.

A just society is organized around certain political principles and values. These are enshrined in constitutions and other foundational documents. Just states also take steps to ensure these values have vitality within the public political culture. We require new immigrants to learn and endorse certain values. We teach these values to students in civics classes. Doing so provides people with the tools to stand up for themselves when they are wronged. However, this also reinforces the recognition that other citizens are equal rights-holders whose independence must be respected alongside our own.

Solidarism of this kind – standing with our fellow citizens – is a political value that requires cultivation. Rawls (1985, p. 152) briefly remarks that 'some public support of art and culture and science, and funding museums and public performances, is certainly vital to the public political culture: to a society's sense of itself and its history, and an awareness of its political traditions.' Following Rawls, I want to sketch three broad ways that a society's history and sense of itself can convert private values associated with the arts into public ones under the idea of solidarity.

Toleration

Most societies contain some level of heterogeneity with respect to religion, ethnicity, and language. These differences are often the basis for cultural and political factionalism. Within multicultural societies, it can be easy to discount others based on their foreign customs with respect to worship, dress, food, and language. Simply pointing to the legally equal status of these customs will not lead a cultural traditionalist toward toleration. The arts can be an effective means for fostering toleration and mutual respect where legalistic norms fail.

Art commonly evokes emotional rather than intellectual responses, and for some people emotional responses are more profound. Films can have this effect.

When we see and hear first person accounts of what it is like to be a member of some ethnic group, we are provided a more personal point of access into the lives of our fellow citizens and the struggles they face. Funding the arts is a way of making possible a sympathetic response that may be less forthcoming when we focus exclusively on formal legal equality. The public value of this response is that it yields improvements in the political culture, specifically in the relation between citizens.

If this empirical hypothesis is sound, the first justification for public funding for the arts is that they provide a distinctive way of promoting toleration between citizens. Utilizing the arts to promote mutual respect helps us avoid what Kymlicka (1996, pp. 191–192) refers to as the 'excessively legalistic understanding of citizenship which neglects the broader social and cultural aspects of membership.' I agree with Dworkin that the arts embody a form of expression of their own. However, to use this point to justify public support we need to show that they provide distinctive means for pursuing political ends. My argument is that through the arts we can strengthen toleration between citizens.

Rectification

The rectification of social injustice is a public end to which everyone can be compelled to contribute. The arts provide a distinctive forum for identifying and rectifying social injustices. Here is one contemporary example that licenses public investment in the arts. The modern commitment to equality in many nations contrasts with a history of inequality and oppression against certain groups. While we can repudiate the actions of past governments, a nation is not distinct from itself at earlier points in time. Those past injustices were committed through the same institutions that we have today. That is why it is appropriate for governments hundreds of years later to issue public apologies for wrongs in which they had no part.

Public apologies are an important component of a nation taking responsibility for its legacy of wrongdoing. Apologies are not sufficient to right the wrong. Another important component is allowing wronged groups to tell their stories. The arts can function as a valuable outlet for addressing historical wrongs. This has personal value for members of the oppressed groups, but it also benefits the culture as a whole. Majorities are in a better position to help minorities if they are aware of the ways that they have been spared the plight of these groups. Funding the arts is a means to creating these cross-cultural connections.

More specifically, public expenditure for museum collections dedicated to Indigenous Peoples and the story of their oppression is one way to help recover their lost history. One of the effects of colonization has been to weaken indigenous culture, including its artistic practices, traditions, and language. While indigenous culture was not completely eradicated, members of those groups are at a disadvantage relative to others in being able to advocate for their presence in society. As such, devoting public funds to strengthening historically wronged cultures is defensible on public grounds.

Identification

While there are many negative elements of a nation's history that can be made salient through art, the same point applies to the positive aspects of a culture. Each nation has its own landmark court decisions, victories in the face of evil, national heroes from the world of athletics, academia, industry, and so on. This leads to a third way we can understand investing in art as investing in the political aspect of our culture.

One aspect of national identity pertains to political culture. Take for example a nation's immigration policies. Canada's notion of citizenship is strongly influenced by its multinational origin. It consists of several founding peoples, the English, the French, the members of the First Nations and the Inuit. Each agreed (although not all at the same time) to confederation on the condition that there be a right to cultural 'distinctness.'[5] Protections are in place for the linguistic and cultural practices of the founding groups, however Canada's ongoing commitment to multiculturalism yields a mosaic conception of citizenship that is explicitly open to addition by new cultures. By design, Canada's immigration policy encourages newcomers to bring their own culture with them, rather than take on a particular identity associated with being Canadian. Other countries will have different histories and different national identities when it comes to immigration.

The reason this supports public funding for the arts as a public end is that, to the extent that there is something distinctive about a country's political identity, this is a part of the public culture. It is part of makes us the 'we' who we are, as opposed to some other country. The arts can provide a way of expressing the distinctive aspects of a nation's political culture.

These brief arguments for public support for the arts overlap with many of the conclusions drawn by Avigail Ferdman in this issue. The justificatory structure, however, follows a different path. The normative work here is done through the premise that citizenship comes bundled with both entitlements to certain treatment and to certain opportunities. The state is the body in charge of making sure that each citizen achieves the status of independence. Intrinsic value is not part of this argument, and state subsidies aimed at realizing intrinsic values would not be justified. Such expenditure remains objectionable even when these subsidies would lead to cross-pollination that makes everyone better off.

Despite this theoretical difference, I believe that we end up supporting similar practices. For example, Ferdman convincingly argues that public funding is required in order to counteract the crowding-out effect. Under-provision of public goods reduces persons' awareness of these goods. Things of value are then at risk of disappearing, creating an impoverished cultural and intellectual environment, which in turn reduces the prospects for flourishing (this volume). On an independence-based account like mine, when the pursuit of one's conception of the good is blocked, one has a reason to complain. Accordingly, the reluctant taxpayer would have no objection to mandatory taxation aimed at ensuring an adequate range of conceptions of the good. One major difference, however, is that for Ferdman establishing variety is primarily a perfectionist rather than an egalitarian concern. My response to Ferdman will be similar to the one I gave to Nagel. Creating a condition that protects each person's independence is not the same thing as creating a society that preserves access to the very best things in the world.

Importantly, these two goals may come apart. When objects of intrinsic value disappear into the hands of the very rich (or disappear altogether) we may flourish less individually and collectively. While this is lamentable, this is not an injustice. There are many things that would benefit humanity that could be realized if only we marshaled the state's resources toward them. However, political society differs from other associations like wildlife preservation societies and wine tasting clubs. Within an involuntary association like the state respect for each person's independence means restricting the kinds of goals, we can coerce everyone to pursue through public institutions. There is no reason to think this will be costless.

Finally, let me address one possible misunderstanding. I have argued that the arts can play a role in increasing solidarity between citizens, and that solidarity is a public end to which all citizens are committed. This does not mean that public support for art should be limited to works that (charitably described) have political content, or (uncharitably described) are simply propaganda. For example, when discussing the political value of toleration I argued that improvements in general levels of toleration can occur whenever we learn more about the distinct cultural practices of other groups. Funding the arts means providing greater access to the various mediums in which people from a wide cultural background can tell their stories. This is a political value related to citizenship even when the stories they tell have no political content.

I have argued that political power should not be used to try to make people better as people, and so we cannot appeal directly to value of the arts within a good life to justify public funding. However there is a legitimate state interest, not in making us into better *people*, but in making us better *citizens*. According to the brief arguments explored here, the arts can be a distinct mode of expression for how a nation understands itself, how it came to be that way, and why it values the things it does. As Kymlicka (p. 174) notes, a 'shared civic identity' is necessary to 'sustain the level of mutual concern, accommodation, and sacrifice that democracies require.' The reluctant taxpayer is fully committed to public expenditure that enables each to live independently alongside others. I have argued that support for the arts is compatible with that mandate.

Notes

1. This character is based off one of Feinberg's examples. See Feinberg (1994).
2. For the purposes of this paper it does not matter whether one adopts a Kantian or Millian view of independence.
3. This is most obvious in the inverse: there are things that are intrinsically bad but this does not mean that it is permissible to ban or discourage them. Nagel himself defends a position similar to this in Nagel (1997).
4. Without knowledge of this convention we would not be able to distinguish these works from something that really is just noise or a pile of rubbish.
5. See Kymlicka (1996, Chapter 9).

Acknowledgments

I would like to thank Christine Korsgaard, T.M. Scanlon, and Arthur Ripstein for comments on an earlier version of this paper. I would also like to thank the anonymous reviewers of this volume for helpful comments.

Disclosure statement

No potential conflict of interest was reported by the author.

References

Dworkin, R. (1985). *A matter of principle*. Cambridge, MA: Harvard University Press.
Feinberg, J. (1994). Not with my tax money: The problem of justifying government subsidies for the arts. *Public Affairs Quarterly, 8*, 101–123.
Ferdman, A. (this issue). Why the intrinsic value of public goods matters. doi:10.1080/1 3698230.2017.1398869.
Kymlicka, W. (1996). *Multicultural citizenship: A liberal theory of minority rights*. Oxford: Oxford University Press.
Kymlicka, W. (2004). Dworkin on freedom and culture. In J. Burley (Ed.), *Dworkin and his critics* (pp. 113–133). Malden, MA: Blackwell.
Nagel, T. (1991). *Equality and partiality*. Oxford: Oxford University Press.
Nagel, T. (1997). Moral conflict and political legitimacy. *Philosophy & Public Affairs, 16*, 215–240.
Rawls, J. (1985). *Justice as fairness: A restatement*. Cambridge, MA: Harvard University Press.

Why the intrinsic value of public goods matters

Avigail Ferdman

ABSTRACT

Existing accounts of public-goods distribution rely on the existence of solidarity for providing non-universal public goods, such as the humanities or national parks. There are three fundamental problems with these accounts: they ignore instances of social fragmentation; they treat preferences for public goods as morally benign, and they assume that these preferences are the only relevant moral consideration. However, not all citizens unanimously require public goods such as the humanities or national parks. Public-goods distribution that is based only on citizens' preferences, therefore, means that non-universal public good are at a constant risk of under-provision, and has negative implications for human flourishing. The paper, therefore, develops a complementary justification for the distribution of public goods, that decouples the distribution of public goods from ad hoc preferences, and grounds the distributive justification in the intrinsic value of these goods. There are three reasons to include intrinsic-value considerations in public-goods distribution: responding to crowding-out effects; promoting shared heritage and cross-fertilization. Finally, the intrinsic-value justification may indirectly promote solidarity. Thus, the intrinsic-value and the solidarity justifications need not be mutually exclusive, rather they can be mutually reinforcing.

Justice in the distribution of public goods is an issue which only recently has begun to attract attention in the political philosophy literature. The lack of a comprehensive account of normative principles for public-goods distribution is worrying, because in its absence, certain important public goods are at risk of constant underfunding or disappearance. This state of precarity has important social implications: it helps to enshrine a social reality which disproportionately leans toward private consumption goods. The opportunity to engage with and appreciate goods such as nature, culture, or artistic achievements comes to depend on the ability to purchase these things on the private market, rather than by making them accessible to the public through national parks, state-funded museums, and public libraries.

When *non-universal* public goods (NUPGs) are concerned, the need for a comprehensive account of distribution becomes even more urgent. NUPGs include language, culture, vibrant cities, conservation areas, arts, the humanities, and basic science. These goods are special because they are not in everyone's direct interest, yet citizens are often required to subsidize them nonetheless. Justifying this sort of state authority is even more urgent in multicultural and fragmented societies, where a shared 'common good' is either limited or non-existent, in which case citizens will not be willing to cross-subsidize each other.

This is not merely a problem of justifying taxation. Rather, the type of public goods the state will provide, or the possibility that it will disinvest altogether, determines the sort of society we live in: whether it will be a society that secures the existence of public spaces or rather privatizes land; whether it will lean toward individualism or toward a shared common good; whether it will promote equal access to valuable goods (arts, nature) or leave them up for grabs.

In this paper, I argue that in order to achieve a comprehensive account of public-goods distribution, we need to replace state-neutrality toward conceptions of the good life with an approach that explicitly accounts for intrinsic value. Precisely because public goods are in the realm of the public, state-neutrality – usually reserved for the private realm (Nagel, 1987) – is conceptually inappropriate for approaching the question of public goods.

Moreover, previous discussions on public-goods distribution appeal to reasons such as solidarity and good-will (Claassen, 2013; Miller, 1999), yet overlook social contexts in which these are weak or absent. Moreover, these accounts attend only to subjective preferences, yet they end up disadvantaging minorities and are, therefore, not conducive to justice. Introducing intrinsic-value reasons for public-goods distributions can circumvent the problems of weak solidarity and disadvantaged minorities in one distributive framework.

I start by motivating the discussion of NUPGs and justice, arguing that NUPGs merit distinct distributive justifications. I map the normative background in which public-goods distribution has been discussed, highlighting the areas that require more theoretical and normative attention. I do this by introducing an analytic distinction between 'subjective-preferences' and 'intrinsic-value' accounts of distribution, showing how the latter, developed in this paper, can complement the former, to provide a comprehensive theory of public-goods distribution.

NUPGs and the distributive problem

The standard economic understanding of public goods is that they are material goods that the private market cannot provide efficiently (Stiglitz, 2000). The collection of essays in this volume, however, provides a richer background for the concept of public goods. The 'public' is thus understood as encompassing non-material public goods as well. For example, the existence of a just society is in itself a public good, a good that the private market will not supply. Normatively, it is desirable that the state foster certain non-material public goods, like a just society, not only because the private market will be less efficient, but because it is intrinsically good even if aggregate individual preferences suggest otherwise.

Very few public goods are perceived by all (reasonable) citizens as serving a basic interest. National security, police protection, and clean air are among these uncontroversial goods that all reasonable persons have reason to support. Most other public goods, however, are not a basic interest in this sense. Vibrant cities, conservation areas, arts, basic science, etc. are goods that do not reflect a basic interest that every person in society has. In addition, even when persons do have an interest in these goods, their degree of interest might not be equal. They might prefer different combinations of these goods, or deny that these goods should be provided by the state. Finally, the absence of these goods does not violate basic justice (Miller & Taylor, forthcoming).

The distributive problem of such NUPGs, for example, the humanities, is that persons who are less interested in the humanities bear more of the cost of its provision compared to persons who gain more benefit from it. It may be the case that some citizens prefer another NUPG, like a network of bicycle lanes. Should bike lovers help pay for the humanities? Do they have a legitimate complaint if they are compelled to pay for the humanities even if they would rather use their taxes for more bike lanes, or for purchasing private goods? I begin by reviewing current liberal accounts of public-goods distribution, and demonstrating how they might lead to unwanted distributive outcomes.

Subjective preferences: existing justifications for distribution of competing NUPGs

Liberal-neutrality accounts of public-goods distribution (Claassen, 2013; Miller, 2004; White, 2003) ground the justification for distribution in a combination of two considerations:

- Demand: the number of people who are interested in a NUPG;
- Cost: the relative cost of a NUPG compared to other state-supported goods.

The distributive question, in these liberal accounts, is how to make necessary tradeoffs among NUPGs which attract different levels of interest among persons, and have varying costs. Implicitly, this is a 'subjective preferences' account of the justice in NUPGs distribution, as it assumes that what matters in determining whether justice has been achieved is whether the allocation of NUPGs corresponds to citizens' aggregate individual preferences. For example, let us imagine two groups: group (A) prefers the humanities and group (B) prefers bicycle lanes. So long as no group or individual express an interest in a third NUPG, e.g. public broadcasting television, the state has no reason to provide it.

Tradeoffs among NUPGs in the subjective-preferences approach are concretized by cross-subsidization. Cross-subsidization is taken to mean that when a certain group (A) prefers NUPG1, while another group (B) prefers NUPG2, group (A) will help support NUPG2 and group (B) will help support NUPG1. This way both groups will receive the NUPG that they prefer. The important conceptual point here is that it is assumed that group (A) prefers only NUPG1 and group (B) prefers only NUPG2. This qualification is important because it is assumed that there are no spill-over effects across the different groups.

Assuming no spill-over effects, cross-subsidization requires a per-capita allocation: in a society in which distinct groups are interested in distinct public goods, providing these goods will be done through general taxes, whereby each tax-paying citizen is supporting not only her preferred NUPGs but other groups' preferred NUPGs as well. Importantly, so long as there are different groups with competing interests in distinct NUPGs, it is morally required that the majority does not impose its preferences on the minority (Claassen, 2013). A per-capita distribution, therefore, allocates NUPGs according to the relative share of groups. For example, if 80% of the population prefers the humanities and the remainder prefers bicycle lanes then the NUPG allocation would follow these proportions. In fact, so long as the NUPGs in question do not violate basic rights and liberties, their content does not really matter. This content-neutrality will become problematic once we learn of the implications of per-capita distributions, discussed shortly.

Per-capita distribution requires solidarity, a sense of majoritarian good-will, or a commitment to rights-based fairness. The more homogenous the society, the higher the degree of willingness to cross-subsidize, and the greater the likelihood that the different groups will make a conscious effort to reduce their demands from extravagant to modest (Miller, 2004). In the absence of solidarity, however, some NUPGs may not be capable of crossing the threshold that is needed for their existence. For example, endangered languages require more support than a national language. Yet without cross-subsidization, its speakers may not be able to acquire sufficient resources to keep the language viable. The absence of solidarity, therefore, weakens the willingness to cross-subsidize leading to under-provision of NUPGs.

In the absence of solidarity, the liberal accounts may turn to justify cross-subsidization by appealing to fairness as even-handed treatment (Patten, 2014). When a majority prefers NUPG1, and a minority prefers NUPG2, the decision on how many units of resources should be allocated between NUPG1 and NUPG2 will be made according to a democratic decision. In order to avoid 'majority tyranny', the majority lends a helping hand to the minority (Claassen, 2013), resulting in a per-capita distribution. Yet the even-handed approach is not problem-free, as follows.

The extension of good-will and the problem of small minorities
A per-capita approach may disadvantage small minorities who may find that their per-capita share is insufficient for covering the cost of their NUPG. To

illustrate: not all minority languages can be encompassed by a multilingual policy, as certain languages do not have enough speakers. There must be a cut-off somewhere and it will inevitably be arbitrary, whether grounded on sheer numbers or on relative power (Weinstock, 2003).

One way to avoid this problem of systematic minority-disadvantage is to over-extend the good-will of the majority. In other words, to provide a higher than per-capita support for small minorities. The justification could go like this: 'it is unfair that small minorities are systematically disadvantaged in a per-capita scheme, so they should receive more resources than a per-capita distribution prescribes'.

This, however, is also problematic. Imagine a majority that prefers team sports and a small minority that prefers experimental physics. The minority wants to build a LIGO-type facility[1] that would cost millions of dollars. Applying the extended good-will argument, the majority has to subsidize the physicists, in virtue of their being a systematically disadvantaged minority. The majority has to accept the minority's preferences and withhold complaints that LIGO is too expensive.

Now let us revise the example, and substitute the physicists with a group of persons whose purpose in life is to count 'blades of grass in variously geomet-rically shaped areas' (Rawls, 1999, p. 380). Let us also assume that providing and maintaining grass fields is very expensive. Can members of the majority legitimately claim that they should not be compelled, as a matter of justice, to support an activity that they view as completely worthless?

According to the extended good-will argument, they cannot. They will have to disproportionately support such activities, even activities they consider wholly worthless or silly, simply because it so happens that a tiny minority is interested in them. Such a distributive principle seems to be licensing too much: any activity that corresponds to subjective preferences will have to be supported, regardless of its value, purpose, or cost. This might strike some as a tyranny of the smallest minority.

Minority preferences as expensive tastes

Another problem with the preference-based approach is that it might end up withholding support for many important public goods. This is because a prefer-ence-based approach may eradicate the distinction between private goods and public goods, disregarding the cultural context and social value of public goods (see Kohn, this volume). When we approach public goods as things that are allocated according to preferences, we treat them, essentially, as consumption goods. This is because the subjective-preferences approach implicitly relies on an 'expensive-tastes' argument. According to the expensive-tastes argument, treating individuals equally requires that each individual receive an equal share of resources (Dworkin, 2000; Patten, 2014) to use according to their best judg-ment. One person may want to purchase consumption goods, another may want to join others and together invest in a collective project. The value of a good (regardless of whether it is private or public) is determined according to its demand on the market: the more people share a 'taste' for a certain good, the lower its cost will be. Persons should be held responsible for their tastes and preferences, and it is, therefore, unfair to demand that others with less expensive tastes subsidize the higher cost of these extravagant preferences (Dworkin, 2000, 2004, pp. 339–350).

The distributive criterion for public goods that follows is: 'any taste that costs above per-capita should not be supported by the state, unless there is an independent reason for state-support'. The caveat is important, because it distinguishes between public goods that are essential for justice (e.g. national security, basic education) and non-essential public goods (NUPGs). So long as a public good is essential for justice, the state may provide it without regard to a per-capita allocation. However, because we are dealing with NUPGs (e.g. parks, libraries, museums) which are not essential for justice, we may not invoke a reason of justice to override the per-capita allocation. The upshot is that according to the expensive-tastes argument, a per-capita distribution is required for state support of NUPGs.

To illustrate, a person can choose to spend her equal share of resources on consumption goods, or she can group with other people and try to realize a collective project, like an institution for experimental physics. However, she may not demand that others support her and her fellow physicists with an above than per-capita share so that they could build the expensive LIGO. The group's own resources will not suffice and they will not be able to build the LIGO. Museums, national parks, and public libraries are likewise expensive and will not be feasible if the group that is interested in them is too small.

The risk with the expensive-tastes argument, originally invoked to ensure that people with average tastes in consumption goods (e.g. beer) do not have to subsidize people with extravagant tastes (e.g. champagne), is that it can be hijacked by a majority that happens not to want to subsidize public goods like national parks, public libraries or humanities departments. Treating such public goods as mere extravagant tastes misses their important social and cultural role. Yet a content-neutral, preference-based approach is conceptually bound to treat libraries, museums, and parks as consumption goods that are dependent on ad hoc tastes. This strengthens the need to introduce distributive considerations that go beyond subjective preferences.

Reasons for including intrinsic-value considerations in public-goods distribution

The preference-based approach should be supplemented by an account of intrinsic value. A thing is intrinsically valuable when it is good in itself, when it is not (merely) instrumental as a means for achieving another good. The criterion for judging when a thing has intrinsic value, adopted in this paper, is derived from human flourishing theories (Hurka, 1993; Sher, 1997). It treats subjective preferences (e.g. hedonistic pleasure, desire satisfaction) as only part of the explanation of what is of value. Briefly, a thing will be judged to be of intrinsic value when it contains the following: knowledge, achievement, loving relationships, moral virtue, and pleasure. These goods have more value when they are combined: things will be judged as intrinsically good when they promote a well-rounded life, and when they cross-fertilize each other, both within an individual and across individuals (Hurka, 2006). Since this essay is concerned with public goods, I restrict the discussion of intrinsic value to institutions or practices that provides opportunity for well-rounded flourishing (and not to particular discrete goods like works of excellent art).

Different NUPGs correspond to different things that have intrinsic value. The opera, for example, provides opportunity for musical knowledge and achievement; bike lanes provide the opportunity for physical achievement, health, and protection of the environment; public libraries provide an opportunity to encounter new ideas. A pluralistic value theory will not rank these intrinsic goods against each other, but it will nevertheless insist that a combination of these goods is better than achieving only one of them (Hurka, 2006).

Of course, intrinsic value exists not only in public goods, but in private goods as well. Does this mean that there is no distinction between these categories? Not necessarily. Compare, for example, a Stradivarius and the symphony. Both have intrinsic value but the symphony can do much more for collective flourishing compared to a Stradivarius. In general, public goods have a normative role that private goods do not have: they are supposed to secure the perpetuation of their intrinsic value, in order to promote human flourishing and to create the conditions for the even spread of the good across persons. The state is responsible for supporting certain public goods precisely because of market failure, because the commodities market will fail at distributing their intrinsic goodness evenly across persons. So while private goods and public goods may both have intrinsic value, the way this value is distributed across persons differs significantly. To the extent that the state is responsible for creating the conditions for leading flourishing lives, it is responsible for the provision of public goods that contribute to flourishing. The following elaborates.

The crowding-out effect

Competition between different types of public goods can drive less popular goods out of existence. If in the competition between grass fields and the humanities the grass fields win, the result is that the *combination* of intrinsic goods that humanities provides – knowledge, aesthetic awareness, meaningful relationship with others, etc. – becomes less viable.

Michael Kessler (this volume) examines the relationship between goods of intrinsic value and the responsibility of society to support them. He considers

Thomas Nagel's argument, which stipulates the following (Nagel, 1991, pp. 132–136):

(1a) Some things, like 'high art', have intrinsic value.
(2a) Reasonable persons will recognize the existence of this intrinsic value.

It follows, therefore, that

(3a) The state should support these things of intrinsic value.

Kessler agrees with Nagel on premises (1) and (2), but rejects the conclusion. According to Kessler, the fact that some things have intrinsic value does not automatically translate to state responsibility to support this value. In other words, reasonable persons can acknowledge the intrinsic worth of high art yet coherently hold that it is not the job of the state to support them, just in virtue of their excellence. As an analogy, consider the intrinsic good of love or friendship. It is not the job of the state to actively promote love or friendship through the distribution of resources (for example, by giving money to happily married couples). Friendship and love are best left for individuals to pursue in their private lives. The implication is that the intrinsic value of art is not enough, by itself, to justify state-support. Other arguments in favor of support need to be given (such as promoting the value of citizenship through arts, as Kessler proposes).

The crowding-out effects of certain public goods provide some support for Nagel's conclusion (3) that the state should (sometimes) fund things of intrinsic value, in virtue of their having intrinsic value, and independent of other instrumental arguments, like the value of citizenship. The difference between Kessler's approach and the intrinsic-value approach is grounded in the varying degree of optimism about the resilience of things of value. Kessler's reluctant tax payer is optimistic about things of intrinsic value: they are excellent enough that someone will support them, through the private market. They will have become someone's expensive taste, and this someone exists and protects high art from disappearing.

My own view is more pessimistic. When things of intrinsic value disappear from our mental map, we are deprived of the opportunity to know or appreciate them. If public libraries disappear from the public sphere, our lives are impoverished. This is true not because we will have to pay for books from our own pockets, but rather because the opportunity to gain knowledge, collectively, is severely diminished. The tax payer, in this scenario, no longer acknowledges the intrinsic value of goods that exist through the institution of the public library, because she lacks the epistemic background to appreciate its value. There is a similar rational for protecting natural environments: it will be difficult to appreciate the Great Barrier Reef or the Dead Sea if they were, for example, to be exploited for natural resources beyond recognition.

Martha Nussbaum (2010) tells the story of the Chicago Children's Choir, as an illustration of the effects of non-exposure to arts and music. Chicago is characterized by huge socioeconomic gaps and deep de facto racial segregation. Chicago public schools suffer from a severe arts budget cut back. The Chicago Children's Choir, a philanthropic organization, has stepped into this void and set up a network of school, neighborhood, and concert choirs that includes 3000 children, 80% of which are below the poverty line. The choir gives the children an unparalleled opportunity for an intense experience side by side with children from different racial, economic, and ethnic background. Also, since the choir members sing music from different cultures, the children connect, expressively and intellectually, with these cultures. By learning music from different times and places they cultivate their curiosity in other persons and in other things. They often become role models for other children in their neighborhoods. Needless to say, Nussbaum continues, these effects multiply across parents, families neighborhoods, and the choirs' audiences.

Being part of a choir is a lived and felt experience. The children train themselves to synchronize their breathing with others, they memorize everything they sing, and involve facial expression, gestures, and dance in their performances. They have to produce sounds from within their body, which at an age where they feel uncomfortable in their bodies gives them an opportunity to develop a sense of ability, discipline, and responsibility (Nussbaum, 2010, chapter 6).

This experience is not something that can be replicated by reading a book about music, humming a tune or forming a band in one's garage. Children who do not have the opportunity to participate in a choir, therefore, are not only deprived of the opportunity to tap into the goods described above. They remain unaware that these goods could even exist for them. To generalize, so long as goods like arts and the humanities are underfunded, they are at risk of being epistemically crowded out. In the future, they will not feature in citizens' preference sets. We can, therefore, restate Nagel's argument to reflect this implication:

(1a) Some things, like 'high-art' genres, have intrinsic value.
(2a) If such things of value disappear, so does the capacity to appreciate them.
(3a) Reasonable persons would (or should) oppose the disappearance of these capacities.
(4a) The commodities market alone will not protect the existence of these things of value (Dworkin, 1985).
(5a) The state should support these things of intrinsic value, otherwise they might disappear.

It follows, therefore, that

(6a) Reasonable persons will then come to recognize the existence of this intrinsic value, and be willing to support them.

The reworked steps show that appreciating things of intrinsic value requires knowing them, in the experiential sense, and this in turn requires state action, through the provision of public goods.

Creating the conditions for good lives

The state has another reason to support intrinsically valuable things when these things help in creating a social environment that promotes human flourishing. Recall the analogy drawn above, between love/friendship and the arts. This analogy was used to show that a liberal would insist that the state should not support things of value simply in virtue of their intrinsic goodness. Yet there is a distinction worth making between a state of affairs in which individuals achieve goods like love or friendship, and a state of affairs in which there are social conditions that enable or hinder the potential for achieving friendship and love. So while it is not the job of the state to interfere in persons' friendships or love-lives, it may very well be the job of the state to create the public environment that will enable people to form meaningful relationships and for example,

> [p]ublic policy can address a culture of anomie or alienation that breeds loneliness; support for a rich and diverse public culture of clubs, festivals and concerts, drop-in centers, nature walks, libraries and swimming pools can provide opportunities for social interaction and community. (Sypnowich, 2014, p. 186)

Waheed Hussain (this volume), invokes a similar argument about the role of institutions in creating an environment supportive of social connectedness. Hussain argues that the structure of resource distribution in extreme competitive markets, like the US, encourages competition between individuals which is anathema to meaningful social relations, because it forces persons to step over each other in order to protect their own interests. Competition is bad, according to Hussain, because it pits persons against each other, eliminating the good of meaningful relationships. On this view, it is very much the job of the state to structure the economic market such that it provides the conditions for more meaningful relationships (intrinsically good) and less competitive, aggressive behavior (intrinsically bad). State intervention through the support of less competitive environments can, therefore, be grounded in two reasons: instrumentally, there are social benefits from eradicating harmful competitive institutions. The second reason is non-instrumental: the intrinsic goodness of friendship, and the goodness inherent in social connectedness are themselves reasons for creating environments that reduce harmful competition.

Using this analogy, it is possible to generalize the scope of state responsibility to the following: the state can legitimately create the conditions for the perpetuation of intrinsically valuable goods, such as the arts, the humanities, basic science, and meaningful social relationships, through the support of libraries, museums, concert halls, nature reserves, and viable public spaces. Note that this does not entail that the state should support all intrinsically valuable goods all of the time. Rather, it provides the state a reason to allow the intrinsic goodness of something to count in its favor in the distributive calculus, when the stakes are high, or when the good in question is at risk of being crowded out.

The shared-heritage argument

Things like great architecture, human languages, and other human achievements are valuable, in part, because they have a collective-agency component: they have been created, appreciated (and criticized) by people in society, often across generations. For example, a language has intrinsic value because it is a human achievement, because it is a representation of complex systems of thought and communication structured over generations (Reaume, 2000).

The shared-heritage argument rests on a similar understanding of the nature of value – its cooperative essence – and adds a non-material component. I argue that since intrinsic value of non-material things like art, knowledge, friendship, etc. is partly due to its cooperative and collective nature, we have reason to recognize this value within distributive calculations.

The story of Stonehenge is illustrative: one of England's most significant monuments was, until 1918, privately owned. In 1915, there were speculations that a wealthy American might buy Stonehenge, dismantle it and transport it abroad. As of 1918 it is owned by the Crown; the grounds surrounding it belong to the National Trust. Imagine that nowadays, Disney Corporation approaches the British government, offering to buy Stonehenge, in order to dismantle it and recreate it in Disneyland, California. The offer is very high and the British government – motivated by an egalitarian sentiment – distributes the proceeds among its citizens in such a way that reduces economic gaps. The shared-heritage argument holds that the British government and the British people have reason to resist the Disney offer because Stonehenge, in its original location, has intrinsic value, which is incommensurable with its instrumental value.

David Miller (2004) also employs the shared-heritage argument, albeit differently, to justify cross-subsidization. Miller argues that a shared heritage provides reason to cross-subsidize, because members in a society recognize the value of belonging to a society, even if they are not interested in supporting particular NUPGs that other members prefer. The shared heritage acts like the social cement, helping to create trust between citizens, which, in turn, is instrumental for the effective administration of social justice (Miller, 1995). For Miller, therefore, the value of shared heritage is instrumental for promoting social justice.

I argue from the opposite direction: the value of the shared heritage is in part due to its intrinsic value. While for Miller heritage can theoretically include anything that performs as the social cement (barring unjust or evil things), the intrinsic-value argument is more discriminatory: it does not provide a blanket justification for any NUPG, but rather to those NUPGs which act as the social cement because they are intrinsically good. More specifically, NUPGs which the state should try to support, shared heritage included, are things that encourage well-rounded lives, and that enable cross-fertilization, as discussed in the following.

The cross-fertilization argument

The final argument in favor of introducing intrinsic-value considerations into distributive tradeoffs is that this has the potential of spreading the value more evenly. In other words, there is an implicit multiplier effect that the subjective-preferences approach does not capture. Recall that the preference-based approach treats each NUPG as reflecting the preferences of one group and one group only. The intrinsic-value approach, in contrast, can account for spill-over effects of NUPGs, such that their distribution may be analyzed in a less artificial manner.

The liberal accounts of NUPGs distribution assume that there is a one-to-one relationship between persons and public goods: distinct NUPGs are treated as if they are in the interest of one group and one group only. Moreover, the literature tends to position NUPG 'lovers' against 'market-good' lovers (Claassen, 2013; Miller, 2004) delineating each distinct group with a distinct preference. Thus, Opera is treated as if only Opera lovers want it, bicycle lanes as if bicycle lovers want them, etc.

This might be a useful simplification for interrogating distributive obligations, yet it misses one of the constitutive features of NUPGs – that they are indeed public. Once these goods are made available, they no longer need to cater only to the interests of the group which initially asked for them. Their very existence can attract new people, and can therefore both promote more flourishing and reduce distributive burdens, since more people will benefit from these goods. Cross-subsidization can therefore become cross-fertilization, where different NUPGs are made more accessible to people who may otherwise not be aware of their existence or of their intrinsic value.

From the point of view of human flourishing this is important, because cross-fertilization invites encounters between people and ideas that may not occur in the absence of certain NUPGs. Thus, encountering a NUPG that one may not have initial interest in may spark one's imagination or invite one to engage in new and different activities. Because public-goods distribution does not have to follow a zero-sum calculation (as entailed by the subjective-preferences approach), the multiplier effect of intrinsic value provides another reason to introduce intrinsic value into the distributive calculus.

Admittedly, some NUPGs are going to be more accessible than others: bicycle lanes are going to be accessible to anyone who has access to a bicycle, whereas the Opera is going to be accessible to people who already have some sort of knowledge, experience and appreciation of this genre (Bourdieu, 1977); nature reserves are going to be more accessible than experimental physics. Yet the Opera or experimental physics have important spill-over effects that may contribute to cross-fertilization indirectly, for example by inspiring interest in popular science.

Spill-over promotes a more egalitarian access to things of intrinsic value. An accessible public library can reach many people, providing them with the intrinsic value of knowledge and aesthetic appreciation. This provides a reason to support a library, compared to a collection of geometrically varied fields of grass, in which there is no growth or intensification of intrinsic value. It also provides a reason for the state to support the library over the option of distributing book-vouchers to individuals. Both options provide access to intrinsic goods, but the institution of the library creates greater and more evenly distributed spill-over compared to the privatized option.

Conclusions

In this paper, I develop a complementary justificatory approach to NUPGs distribution that can account for non-solidaristic social contexts, and thus contributes to a more comprehensive framework for public-goods distribution. The most distinctive feature of the intrinsic-value approach compared to previous accounts of justice in public-goods distribution is that it breaks with the liberal commitment to neutrality toward conceptions of the good. The new approach explicitly attends to the intrinsic value of the goods that should be supported by the state.

NUPGs do more than merely create distributive benefits and burdens. They are also agents of socialization. They perform an important role in creating and upholding the institutions through which we come to shape, revise, and change our conceptions of the good life and our conceptions of human flourishing (Galston, 2010). Therefore, determining which NUPGs deserve more support than other NUPGs is not only a matter of resource allocation that corresponds to preferences. Rather, it is an engagement in shaping society and culture. Precisely because NUPGs are public goods, they enable access not only to those who initially demand them but to a wider population.

Thus support for the humanities, for example, influences public discourse, raises awareness to different points of view and modes of thinking. It creates a public environment very different from an environment in which the humanities are not supported, or confined to the connoisseurs, as the Chicago Children's Choir demonstrates. NUPGs distribution should not be merely an exercise in justice as preference-satisfaction. It is an exercise in the distribution of the theoretical and practical resources that persons are equipped with to engage with the world. The potential for cross-fertilization and the role of NUPGs as socialization agents invite us to treat NUPG distribution not as a framework for adjudicating between competing, incompatible goods, but rather for determining which NUPGs serve the interest of human flourishing.

Introducing intrinsic-value considerations to public-goods distribution no doubt invites complications, compared to the more straightforward preference-based approach. In the preference-based approach we only have to count heads, while in the intrinsic-value approach we have to include judgments about the relative value of different NUPGs. There is no straightforward recipe for doing this, but two points are nevertheless worth mentioning.

First, recall that generally speaking, goods are valuable when they promote well-rounded lives and allow for cross-fertilization. This does provide a rough rule of thumb, although hard cases remain when different NUPGs may demonstrate a similar potential to promote well-rounded lives and cross-fertilization. Adjudicating between these goods will then require an independent distributive criterion, such as even-handed treatment, equality, or efficiency. Yet these independent criteria are introduced after intrinsic-value considerations have been weighed. This is significantly different from a subjective-preferences approach in which intrinsic value might not be considered at all. Second, despite the indeterminacy in hard cases, the introduction of intrinsic-value considerations is meant to break the mold of preference-based, liberal-neutrality distributive approaches that refrain from taking a stand on what is good, and to create a space for a deliberative discourse in which persons can reason and argue about the value of different things in a comprehensive, informed manner.

Finally, there is an important connection between solidarity and NUPGs. Previous sections argue that solidarity cannot be the only justification for cross-subsidization of NUPGs, for the simple fact that such a justification neglects ubiquitous contexts of social strife and social divisions. In the discussion above I argue for an alternative justification for NUPGs distribution that does not depend on the existence of solidarity. Yet I would like to argue that one does not have to exclude the idea of solidarity altogether from the discussion of NUPGs distribution. Given the potential for cross-fertilization discussed above, support for different types of NUPGs that have intrinsic value may actually prove to promote solidarity. Having access to, engaging with and experiencing different NUPGs that one might initially not have been interested in, and seeing others engaging with new NUPGs, might help to promote a sense of having shared non-political values (Kallhoff, 2014).

Thus, NUPGs play an epistemic role by raising awareness to different ideas, lifestyles and people. I.M. Young argued that physical separation can make persons oblivious to injustice (Young, 2000). Physical desegregation, therefore, plays an important epistemic role in making people aware of injustice. In a similar vein, having access to different NUPGs may raise awareness and appreciation of the ideas, values, and pursuits that they embody, and thus help to strengthen solidarity. Thus, the intrinsic value of NUPGs and the solidarity justifications need not be mutually exclusive, but can rather be mutually reinforcing.

Note

1. Laser Interferometer Gravitational-wave Observatory (LIGO) are detectors for measuring ripples in the fabric of spacetime – gravitational waves.

Acknowledgments

I am very grateful to Margaret Kohn and Michael Kessler and to the participants of the 'Approaches to Public Goods: Solidarity and Social Justice' workshop at the Center for Ethics, University of Toronto, May 13–14, 2016. The workshop was made available by the Social Sciences and Humanities Research Council of Canada, The Munk School of Global Affairs, University of Toronto and the Department of Political Science, University of Toronto.

Disclosure statement

No potential conflict of interest was reported by the author.

ORCID

Avigail Ferdman http://orcid.org/0000-0002-0950-8762

References

Bourdieu, P. (1977). *Reproduction in education, society and culture*. London: Sage.

Claassen, R. (2013). Public goods, mutual benefits, and majority rule. *Journal of Social Philosophy, 44*(3), 270–290.

Dworkin, R. (1985). *A matter of principle*. Cambridge, MA: Harvard University Press.

Dworkin, R. (2000). *Sovereign virtue*. Cambridge, MA: Harvard University Press.

Dworkin, R. (2004). Ronald Dworkin replies. In J. Burley (Ed.), *Dworkin and his critics* (pp. 339–395). Malden, MA: Blackwell.

Galston, W. A. (2010). Realism in political theory. *European Journal of Political Theory, 9*(4), 385–411.

Hurka, T. (1993). *Perfectionism*. New York, NY: Oxford University Press.

Hurka, T. (2006). Value theory. In D. Copp (Ed.), *The Oxford handbook of ethical theory* (pp. 357–379). New York, NY: Oxford University Press.

Hussain, W. (this volume). Why should we care about competition?

Kallhoff, A. (2014). Why societies need public goods. *Critical Review of International Social and Political Philosophy, 17*(6), 635–651.

Kessler, M. (this volume). Engaging the reluctant taxpayer.

Kohn, M. (this volume). Solidarity and social rights.

Miller, D. (1995). *On nationality*. Oxford: Clarendon Press.

Miller, D. (1999). Social justice and environmental goods. In A. Dobson (Ed.), *Fairness and futurity: Essays on environmental sustainability and social justice* (pp. 151–172). Oxford: Oxford University Press.

Miller, D. (2004). Justice, democracy and public goods. In K. Dowding, R. E. Goodin, & C. Pateman (Eds.), *Justice and democracy: Essays for Brian Barry* (pp. 127–149). Cambridge: Cambridge University Press.

Miller, D., & Taylor, I. (forthcoming). Distributive justice and public goods. In S.Olsaretti (Ed.), *The Oxford handbook of distributive justice*. Oxford: Oxford University Press.

Nagel, T. (1987). Moral conflict and political legitimacy. *Philosophy & Public Affairs, 16*(3), 215–240.

Nagel, T. (1991). *Equality and partiality*. Oxford: Oxford University Press.

Nussbaum, M. C. (2010). *Not for profit: Why democracy needs the humanities*. Princeton, NJ: Princeton University Press.

Patten, A. (2014). *Equal recognition: The moral foundations of minority rights*. Princeton, NJ: Princeton University Press.

Rawls, J. (1999). *A theory of justice* (revised ed.). Cambridge, MA: Harvard University Press.

Reaume, D. G. (2000). Official-language rights: Intrinsic value and the protection of difference. In W. Kymlicka & W. Norman (Eds.), *Citizenship in diverse societies* (pp. 245–272). Oxford: Oxford University Press.

Sher, G. (1997). *Beyond neutrality: Perfectionism and politics*. Cambridge: Cambridge University Press.

Stiglitz, J. E. (2000). *Economics of the public sector* (3rd ed.). New York, NY: W. W. Norton.

Sypnowich, C. (2014). A new approach to equality. In D. Weinstock & R. Merrill (Eds.), *Political neutrality: A reevaluation* (pp. 178–209). Basingstoke: Palgrave Macmillan.

Weinstock, D. M. (2003). The antinomy of language policy. In W. Kymlicka & A. Patten (Eds.), *Language rights and political theory* (pp. 251–270). New York, NY: Oxford University Press.

White, S. (2003). *The civic minimum: On the rights and obligations of economic citizenship*. Oxford: Oxford University Press.

Young, I. M. (2000). *Inclusion and democracy*. New York, NY: Oxford University Press.

Index

Note: Page numbers in *italics* and **bold** refer to figures and tables respectively.

action-in-concert, politics as 4, 48–50
activism: as compensation 17–18, 20, 22; environmental justice 11, 12, 16–18, 19, 22; racial social solidarity 45, 47
Adorno, T. 64
affirmation: mutual 28–33, *30*, 37–38, 40; unilateral 23n6
antiblack racism 43–48
anti-racist groups 54
Arendt, H. 62
Aristotle 21, 68
arts 6, 102–116; choice and culture 103, 106–111; and citizenship 103, 104, 111–15; intrinsic value 103, 104–106, 124–125; taxpayer's challenge 102–104
autonomy: justice as a claim to (social) property 5–6, 87, 88, 96–98; Kant's moral theory 61; social rights 5, 77–78, 80, 81, 82, 83, 84

Balfour, L. 45
Belle Époque 1, 2, 7
Berger, P. 65
bio-digesters 13–15, 17, 21–22, 23
black solidarity as common oppression 43–47
Bourgeois, L. 2, 76, 99n6
brownfields remediation, environmental justice in 4, 10–24; individual responsibility for environmental justice 16–18; justice of environmental justice 11–13; Louisville's methane 13–15; solidarity 18–22

Canada: citizenship 114; social rights 72, 81
capitalism: justice as a claim to (social) property 6, 88–90, 91, 93, 95; racial structural solidarity 42, 54; and solidarism 74, 75, 87, 95; undermining of solidarity 61, 65, 67, 69
Catholic Social Teaching 2
charity, and the welfare state 95–96
Chicago Children's Choir 124–125, 129
citizenship, and art 103, 104, 111–115
civic solidarity 2
Coates, T.-N. 42
Cohen, C. 45
Cohen, G. A. 74
community capabilities 12, 15, 22–23
compensation: activism as 17–18, 20, 22; social rights 82
competition 3–4, 26–40; instrumental view of social connectedness 27, 34–37; intrinsic value of public goods 126; mutual affirmation conception of social connectedness 28–33; noninstrumental view of social connectedness 27, 37–39; social union conception of social connectedness 27–28, 29; sphere of, and public goods 33–34
Comte, A. 2
conceptualization 65–66
constitutional patriotism 67
cross-fertilization argument, intrinsic value of public goods 128–129, 130
cross-subsidization 119–120, 127, 128, 130
crowding-out effect 123–126
culture and arts 6, 102–116; choice and culture 103, 106–111; and citizenship 103, 104, 111–115; intrinsic value 103, 104–106, 124–125; taxpayer's challenge 102–104

debt, and solidarism 75–76
deference, and solidarity 21, 22

dependence, interpersonal 59–61, 62–63, 67
distribution, and environmental justice 12, 15, 22–23
distributive justice 2, 3; and environmental justice 21
Donzelot, J. 75
Douglass, F. 47, 48–49
Durkheim, É.: self-dissolution 5, 59, 63–65, 67, 68; self-transcendence 69
Dworkin, R.: competition 27, 37; external resources, equality of 93; luck egalitarianism 91; public funding for the arts 103–104, 106–111, 113

economic inequality 1–2
egalitarianism: luck *see* luck egalitarianism; relational 88, 90, 91, 92–93, 97
Encyclopédie Commercial 2
enforced heterosexuality 52, 53
England, Stonehenge 127
environmental justice: brownfields remediation 4, 10–24; individual responsibility 16–18; justice of 11–13
epistemology, and environmental justice 12–13, 15, 16, 18, 23
equality, and social rights 73
equity, solidarity as 20–22, 23
esteem, and interpersonal dependence 60
evil, radical 59, 61–63, 67
expensive tastes 121–122

Fabre, C. 77, 78, 82, 96
Feinberg, J. 116n1
feminism: childcare 45–46; feminist groups 52
Foot, P. 22
Fouillée, A. 2, 75, 93
France: *Belle Époque* 1, 2; revolution 2; solidarism 74
Fraser, N. 12
Freeden, M. 74
Fricker, M. 12

Gaus, G. 88, 98–99n1
gender: and childcare 45–46; racial structural solidarity 45; as seriality 50–52, 55; and sexism 45–46
Gewirth, A. 76, 78, 96, 97
Glover, J. 64
Goffman, E. 60
Goodin, R. 83
Gooding-Williams, R. 4, 43, 45, 47–50, 53

good-will 118, 120–121
Green, T. H. 74

Habermas, J. 67, 69
Hacking, I. 48, 49, 50
health care 27, 33–34, 35, 36, 38–39
Hegel, G. W. F. 61
heritage, shared 127–128
heterosexuality, enforced 52, 53
high art/culture 107–112, 124, 125
Hitler, A. 64
Hobbes, T. 59
Hobhouse, L. 74
Hobson, J. A. 74
Horkheimer, M. 64
Hume, D. 20

ideal theory 3, 74, 79, 80
identification, and the arts 114–115
identity-based solidarity models 67–69
ideology-based solidarity models 67, 68, 69
indeterminacy, and environmental justice 12, 13, 15, 16, 18, 22, 23
India, social rights 72
inequality 3; economic inequality 1–2; racial 42; wealth 45, 46–47
International Covenant on Economic, Social, and Cultural Rights 72
interpersonal dependence 59–61, 62–63, 67
intrinsic value of public goods 6–7, 117–131; cross-fertilization argument 128–129; crowding-out effect 123–126; good lives, creating the conditions for 126–127; public funding of the arts 103, 104–106, 114; shared-heritage argument 127–128; subjective preferences 119–122, 130

Johnson, C. 42
justice: as claim to (social) property 5–6, 87–99; of environmental justice 11–13; equity as core of 20–21; instrumental view of social connectedness 34–37; intrinsic value of public goods 117, 118–119, 122; Kantian 20; luck egalitarianism 79; natural duty of 16; noninstrumental view of social connectedness 39, 40; physical desegregation and obliviousness to injustice 130; reluctant taxpayer 111; state neutrality 102; *see also* distributive justice; environmental justice; social justice

Kant, I.: abstract universalism of Kantian philosophy 2; equity 20, 21; justice

20; radical evil 5, 59, 61–63, 67, 68; social rights 73, 83; social theory 63; solidarism 74

Klu Klux Klan 3

Korsgaard, C. 78

Kymlicka, W. 68, 113, 115

language: and art, analogy between 107–108, 109; intrinsic value 127

left-libertarianism: 5–6, 88, 90–91, 92–95, 98; social rights 74

Levinas, E. 5, 59, 65–66, 67, 68

liberal democracy: competition 3, 26, 27, 33, 34–35; undermining of solidarity 65, 67, 68, 69

liberal egalitarianism 88, 94–98; justice as claim to (social) property 5–6; luck *see* luck egalitarianism; relational 88, 90, 91, 92–93, 97

liberal multiculturalism 68

liberal nationalism 67–68

liberal theory 3, 74; left-libertarianism *see* left-libertarianism; social rights 5, 72–73, 76, 77–81, 83, 84; right-libertarianism 5–6, 88–90, 91–93, 98

Locke, J. 75, 83, 90, 91, 93, 99n3

Louisville, Kentucky 13–16, 17, 19, 21–22, 23

luck egalitarianism: justice as a claim to (social) property 88, 90, 91, 92–93, 94, 97, 99n6; social rights 74, 79

Machiavelli, N. 59

Macpherson, C. B. 98

Marshall, T. H. 96

Marx, K. 27, 60, 72–73

May, L. 20

methane plants 13–16, 17, 21–22, 23

Miller, D. 67, 127

minorities: expensive tastes 121–122; small 120–121

moral spectatorship 59, 65–66, 67, 68–69

mutual affirmation 28–33, *30*, 37–38, 40

Nagel, T. 103, 104–106, 109, 115, 124, 125

nationalism 68–69

Nazis 19, 64

neoliberalism 7, 81

Nietzsche, F. 59

Nikolai, G. 58

non-foundational solidarity 47–50

non-universal public goods (NUPGs) 3; intrinsic value 118–119, 122–130; subjective preferences 119–122

Nussbaum, M. 12, 124–125

Obama, B. 81

Otto, R. 64

participation, and environmental justice 12, 15, 17, 22–23

Piketty, T. 1, 7

Plato 68

Polanyi, K. 65

political relationship 27, 28–29, 37–40

political solidarity 2

popular art/culture 107–108, 110–111

practical-inert realities 51–52, 53, 54

property: dimensions of 88–89, **89**; justice as a claim to 87–99

public goods: competition 33–34; environmental justice 10, 21; solidarism 81; theory and politics of 1–7; *see also* intrinsic value of public goods

racial structural solidarity 4, 42–55; Gooding-Williams on non-foundational solidarity 47–50; race as seriality 53–54; Shelby on black solidarity as common oppression 43–47; Young on seriality and gender as seriality 50–51

racial structure: of labour 53–54; of law 53, 54

racism 43–48, 54; environmental justice 12, 18

radical evil 59, 61–63, 67

radical inequality, and environmental justice 16

Radical Republicans 2

rational choice paradigm 36

Rawls, J.: arts 112; liberal approach to social rights 77, 84; political liberalism 96; racial structural solidarity 44; social union 27–28, *30*; solidarity 67

reciprocity, and instrumental view of social connectedness 34–35

recognition, and environmental justice 12, 15, 22–33

rectification, and the arts 113–114

relational egalitarianism 88, 90, 91, 92–93, 97

religion, and self-dissolution 63–64, 67

Renouvier, C. 74

rent, and solidarism 75–76, 83

Ricardo, D. 76

right-libertarianism 5–6, 88–90, 91–93, 98

Risse, M. 99n7

Rousseau, J.-J.: competition 27, 40n3; interpersonal dependence 5, 59–61, 62–63, 67, 68; public goods 3; social rights 84

sacralization/the sacred 63–65, 67
Sanders, B. 42
Sartre, J.-P.: Jewishness 48; seriality 50–52
Schaeffer, M. 58
Schlosberg, D. 11–12, 15, 20, 22
Scholz, S. 2, 4
self-dissolution 59, 63–65, 67, 68
self-transcendence 69
seriality: gender as 50–52, 55; race as 53–54, 55
sexism 45–46
sexual division of labour 52
shared heritage 127–128
Shelby, T. 4, 43–47, 48, 49, 50
Shklar, J. 68
Shrader-Frechette, K. 16–17, 22
Shue, H. 77
slavery 44, 46–47, 49, 53–54, 82
social, meaning of 73
social connectedness 26, 27, 40, 126; instrumental view 27, 34–37, 38; mutual affirmation conception 28–33; noninstrumental view 27, 37–39, 40; social union conception 27–28, 29
social democracy 27, 65
socialism 73, 74, 99n8
social justice: distribution 12; rectification of injustice through the arts 113–114; shared heritage 127
social liberalism 74
social property: justice as a claim to 87–99; social rights and solidarity 74–77, 80–81, 82–83, 84
social rights and solidarity 5, 72–84; critiques and comparisons 80–83; justice as a claim to (social) property 87, 94, 95–98; liberal approach to 77–80; social property and solidarism 74–77
social solidarity 2
social structure 73
social union 27–28, 29, 30
solidarism: justice as a claim to (social) property 87–88, 93–99; and left-libertarianism 93–95; and liberal egalitarianism 95–98; social rights 5, 73, 74–77, 80–83, 84
solidarity: arts funding 104, 112, 115; civic 2; deontological 21–22; environmental justice 11, 18–22; as equity 20–22, 23; identity-based models 67–69; ideology-based models 67, 68, 69; intrinsic value of public goods 118, 120, 130; meanings 2–3, 18–22; mutual affirmation 29, 32, 40; non-foundational 47–50; objective perspective 58; political 2; as political action on others' terms

19–20, 21; relational approach 19, 21; social 2; subjective perspective 58; teleological approach 18–19, 21; theory and politics of 1–7; uses and threats 57–59; *see also* racial structural solidarity; social rights and solidarity; undermining of solidarity
South Africa, social rights 72
spectatorship, moral 59, 65–66, 67, 68–69
Stilz, A. 20
Stonehenge 127
structure/agency, and environmental justice 13, 15, 16, 18, 23
Sypnowich, C. 126

Tamir, Y. 67
Tax, M., *Rivington Street* 52
taxpayers: intrinsic value of public goods 118, 119, 120; reluctant 6, 102–116, 124; social rights 73, 80
toleration, and the arts 112–113, 115
Tolsma, J. 58

undermining of solidarity 5, 57–69; Durkheim and self-dissolution 63–65; implications for contemporary political theory 67–69; Kant and radical evil 61–63; Levinas and moral spectatorship 65–66; Rousseau and interpersonal dependence 59–61; uses and threats of solidarity 57–59
unilateral affirmation 23n6
United Kingdom, Stonehenge 127
United States: Chicago Children's Choir 124–125, 129; Louisville, Kentucky 13–16, 17, 19, 21–22, 23; primary elections for Democratic Party nominee 42; race 43–50, 53–54; social rights 72, 82
unsocial sociability 62

Van der Meer, T. 58
van Parijs, P. 74, 80

Waldron, J. 89–90
wealth inequality 45, 46–47
welfare state: social rights 83; solidarism 95–96
well-being 76–79
Wiggins, D. 20, 22
world ownership 76, 909–4

Yack, B. 68
Young, I. M.: environmental justice 12; physical desegregation and injustice 130; seriality and gender as seriality 4, 43, 50–52, 55